W9-BRM-516

A Lovable Clown

When I washed my hair, he always sat on the wash basin, one leg around each side of a faucet, and dabbled in the lather. Together we scrubbed my head.

While I took a bath, he occasionally ran off with the soap—just to tease more than anything else . . .

The last laugh was mine, though, for he never failed to fall in at least once before I finished my bath.

You'd scold Frosty? Not much use. He'd sit there and take it like a trooper, both hands covering his eyes . . . And as soon as you stopped speaking, he'd move one finger just a tiny bit so he could peek out and see if it was safe to carry on from there.

"There should be room beside Sterling North's *Rascal* for this wholly captivating book . . . It is impossible to read this winning story without sharing the author's affection for the raccoon . . ."

Publishers Weekly

Most Archway Paperbacks are available at special quantity discounts for bulk purchases for sales promotions, premiums or fund raising. Special books or book excerpts can also be created to fit specific needs.

For details write the office of the Vice President of Special Markets, Pocket Books, 1230 Avenue of the Americas, New York, New York 10020.

FROSTY

A Raccoon To Remember

Harriett E. Weaver

With Illustrations by Jennifer Owings Dewey

AN ARCHWAY PAPERBACK
Published by POCKET BOOKS • NEW YORK

An Archway Paperback published by
POCKET BOOKS, a division of Simon & Schuster, Inc.
1230 Avenue of the Americas, New York, N.Y. 10020

Copyright © 1973 by Harriett E. Weaver

Published by arrangement with Chronicle Books

All rights reserved, including the right to reproduce
this book or portions thereof in any form whatsoever.
For information address Chronicle Books, 54 Mint
Street, San Francisco, Calif. 94103

ISBN: 0-671-64088-7

First Archway Paperback printing July, 1974

23   22   21   20   19   18

AN ARCHWAY PAPERBACK and colophon are
registered trademarks of Simon & Schuster, Inc.

Printed in the U.S.A.

IL 5+

To my father, James R. Weaver (1878-1952) who started the whole raccoon thing for me. Of an evening during the cold Iowa winters when I was very young, he held me spellbound with stories of coons he had known.

Small wonder that I should find myself helpless before the charms of one little character known as Frosty.

1

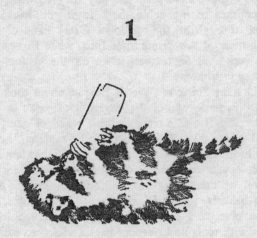

"HERE COMES THE coon's mama!" a youngster called to his family, indicating me with a jerk of his thumb. As of that moment I ceased to be an individual in my own right and began playing second fiddle to a wild animal baby no larger than a mother cat's fuzzy month-old kitten. Funny thing was that I loved it.

Now, not everyone can play second fiddle to a raccoon. You aren't always given the opportunity. If you are camping, he may emerge from the depths of the forest to steal your food. If you happen to live in the forest, as I did, he will call on you regularly and beg for a handout. But not many people become hopelessly adopted. I was. That is, until a certain night, I was.

But in the beginning, to the thousands of folk who came to vacation in this big California redwood state park, I was less a lady ranger than a ways and means of wangling a visit with Frosty. Once in his clutches, how they fussed and gurgled and cooed over him.

You should have seen the way they crowded onto the porches of my cabin, both front and back, and peered through all the windows. Every pane of glass was a mess of noseprints from June, when Frosty took me over, until September, when all the visitors with children went home.

Did I say "took me over"? He just about took over the entire park, one of the largest state parks in California: Big Basin, a truly majestic stand of coast red-wood giants 67 miles south of San Francisco, nestled deep in the Santa Cruz Mountains. More than a million people a year come here from everywhere on earth to marvel at these very old, tall, massive trees. Many bring baskets of food, red-checked tablecloths, and coffee pots, and picnic all day; others come loaded down with tents and sleeping bags and set up camp in one of the park's many inviting campsites for a week or two. Together, they manage to stuff the huge green garbage cans full to overflowing. It's plain to see why the deer and raccoons have always looked upon Big Basin as Heaven on Earth!

What amazed me over the years was the number of campers who actually didn't know what a coon was. I remember especially one frightened lady who pounded on my door in the middle of the night and breathlessly exclaimed that a *monkey* was loose in her camp. "He stands on his hind legs, and I'm sure he's going to spring at my throat," she panted.

Well, I dressed, picked up my big flashlight, and went down to her camp with her. Sure enough, there in the ring of light from her Coleman lantern was not only her "monkey" but his brother, and they were both interested in standing on their hind legs. After all, two people giving them undivided attention would be twice as good as just one. They were so eager to play One-Way Catch with us that they were almost dancing from one foot to the other in anticipation, their eyes gleaming out of those black masks they wore.

"See!" the woman exclaimed, "they're getting ready to jump at us!"

I nearly laughed aloud. "They aren't, really," I assured her, "but they *are* paying a social call. Let's entertain them."

"Entertain them?"

"Sure. It'll be fun. Do you have any leftover bread or cookies or fruit?"

For a moment the camper stared at me as if I weren't quite bright. Then, without a word, she went to her food locker beside the barbecue pit and selected several stale rolls and a chunk of angelfood cake.

"They'll love these," I said, tearing one of the rolls into pieces.

For the next hour—in the dead of night—I showed my new friend what her "monkeys" had in mind. We tossed and they caught until there wasn't anything left in the food locker to play catch with.

By this time the camper had become so completely enchanted with her visitors that she could hardly wait for morning so that she could buy more groceries for them. The way she spent her vacation money on day-old bakery goods, it's a wonder our garbage can cafeterias didn't go out of business! And she even took to sleeping a lot in the daytime, so she could be more nocturnal. The afternoon she finally pulled up stakes and left for home, she told me that this vacation was the first contented one she'd had since her husband died, several years earlier, and furthermore, she announced, she'd be back next summer with a station wagon full of hors d'oeuvres for the Big Basin natives. And she did, too. "I only wish I could take one of the darlings home," she confided, just before she drove away.

I knew how the woman felt. Hadn't I wanted one for my own all the eighteen years I'd been a summer ranger on the crews of the state redwood parks? Before Frosty came to me, people used to ask, "Why don't you grab one of those coons that come to visit you, and keep it for a pet?"

The answer was simple. In the first place I valued my hands very highly; in the second, I didn't want to steal a little coon from his family and make a wretched prisoner of him. Yet I always wished that somehow one would *choose* to come and live with me. But none ever did.

Instead, I had to be content with the furry mob of as many as twenty coons that rumbled in—and always out—of my kitchen in the evenings. It was good to know, however, that they weren't afraid to come into my home—sometimes on winter evenings; that they'd even come clear into my living room and sit around my pot-bellied stove and share late snacks with me.

Only one of them ever abused my hospitality, and had to be banished from the family circle. I was right behind him, too, when he made that scrambling exit, for in one of his hands he clutched my pearls; in the other, my charm bracelet. The rest of the coons, now, made no move to explore my bedroom and get into my personal things. And by midnight they were always ready to troop out and disappear into the cold darkness of the giant forest.

I loved these friends of mine. Each was as individual as any human; each had a personality that was his alone, and that included a healthy amount of mischief. But all of them combined couldn't possibly have caused the uproar that one little coon, named Frosty, was later to create all by himself.

When I first saw him I had no inkling of such utter pandemonium, of course. He was so tiny and frightened. A nine-year-old boy had come to my cabin door and was standing there, snuggling him inside his jacket. "A tree fell on his family," the youngster explained. "I saw it. This one's the only one left. I had to bring him in."

I knew Gary well. He had been coming to Big Basin with his parents every summer for years. In that time he had been on countless nature hikes with me. He had listened to many campfire talks on the inhabitants of the redwood forest; and he had learned that because their mothers are usually not far away, you leave baby wild animals where you find them. Now he was looking at me with misery in his eyes for what I must be thinking. "I had to take care of him," he explained earnestly. "There was no one else."

"Of course you did, Gary," I assured him sympathetically. "Come on in and tell me about it."

There was no doubt that this boy had just received a terrific shock. The natural toppling of a tree in a forest such as this is an earth-shaking experience, never to be forgotten by anyone who witnesses it. Then to find out that the dying giant had destroyed some of our coons was almost too much to bear. Fighting tears, he looked down into the cute, masked face of the catastrophe's only survivor—a tiny wild thing who was now without his loved ones. "This is the first time I've ever touched a coon. I wish he were mine," Gary murmured wistfully, stroking the soft fur around the coon's ears.

"I know," I said, understanding just how he felt. "Now make yourself comfortable in that big chair there, and tell me how you were able to pick him up."

A few minutes passed before Gary could put it all into words. Then, in a low voice that trembled, he said, "It was awful, Miss Weaver, the way the big tree

fell—the noise and everything. It was like in a bad storm and then an earthquake. The little coon's family just disappeared."

I could see that Gary was finding the memory of it painful to remember, and I waited silently until he was able to go on with his account.

"The ground shook, and redwood limbs and needles fell for a long, long time. Then it got awful quiet out there in the forest. I couldn't move, I was so scared. Then I heard a sort of cry, and in a minute, there he was. There I was, too, his first human. He had no mother to run to for help."

"What did you do?" I asked.

"Well," Gary continued, after taking a deep breath, "I sat down in the trail and started talking to him real easy-like."

"Did he come to you?"

"No, not at first. He backed off from me. Then he began to cry some more—louder and louder all the time. Then, all of a sudden—just like that—he came wobbling toward me."

"His legs aren't very steady yet," I told him.

"They sure aren't," Gary agreed, smiling wanly, "and you know? He seemed glad when I took him in my hands and held him close to me. I think it made him feel safe."

I couldn't help noticing Gary's hands. They were rather square, and you couldn't have called them good-looking, but they were gentle, and they were giving one small coon confidence that these humans were going to be all right; they told him that, even though he was now an orphan, someone cared and was going to take care of him.

"He can't be very old," Gary said.

For a moment I studied the furry body. "A month, maybe five weeks, I imagine. A coon kit's eyes aren't open for about three weeks. He probably was born about the middle of May."

"Look at him shiver," the boy said, carefully wiping some dew from the fur on top of the coon's head. "He looked like he had some frost on him when I picked him up. It was cold out there this morning. Okay, Frosty, don't be afraid. We'll take care of you and get you warm." Brightening with a new thought, he added, "Let's call him Frosty."

"It's a good name," I answered, smiling at his pleasure over the idea.

As Gary continued holding the little fellow tight against him to ease his trembling, I thought, "This lad will some day be a man of the forest. He understands wild ones, and they sense his love for them. As much as he's heard us talk about leaving wild babies where they are, he still has the good judgment to know when it is right to bring one in for care. Bless him for that, and for his warm heart."

"I wish he were mine," he said again. I could feel his enormous yearning. I could see what courage it had taken for him to bring the little coon to me, knowing that he would then have to give him up. My heart went out to him.

"Gary," I said softly, "where do you live?"

"In San Francisco," he replied miserably. "I know I couldn't keep him, even if you could let me. He's got to live in a forest or a stream bottom, and go wild when the time comes. But I wish he were mine. I can't help it. I just do."

"Until the war, my home was in Southern California," I told him, "in a small town in orange-and-lemon country. I taught there. Now, in a year or so—after I complete the writing I'm working on—I want to return to my school. But even in a small town like that one, do you know how long a coon pet would last? Do you know how many boys around there have rifles and just one thought in mind—to kill every wild thing they can find? Only a person who lives out in the country or next to a game preserve would stand a chance of raising an animal such as this."

Gary's eyes widened. "Well then, what will become of . . ." His voice trailed off.

I hurried to reassure him. "Don't worry, son," I said quietly, "you saved this baby coon's life. Now I'll see what I can do to get him back to his natural home alive."

"You'll not cage him or—or let him get shot?"

"You can be sure I won't, Gary," I promised. "For a time this cabin will have to be his world, but as soon as he's old enough to look after himself and wants to be free, he will be. One way or another he will be. That's the way you and I believe."

Gary nodded solemnly and after a moment added, "This summer I've decided I'm going to be a ranger when I grow up. Then I can have all the wild animals I want. And they'll be live ones, too, who come to see me like your coons and deer do you—not dead ones I've shot. Maybe I'll join the Fish and Wildlife Service or be a game warden like Mr. Noel. But I'll be something like that anyhow."

"Whichever service gets you, Gary, will be fortunate," I predicted, and I meant it.

So the boy left the tiny coon with me that morning, promising to come back to play with him every day until his vacation was over. But his vacation ended much sooner than he expected, for his father was called home on business.

The night before his family broke camp, Gary came to hold his coon for the last time. Tears glistened in his eyes when he said goodbye. But his eyes shone **as he** talked about the day Frosty would go wild and once again be with his own kind.

Many years have passed since that night. Gary is now grown, and within him must be the same fine warmth and understanding that he showed that summer when he thought more of a coon's welfare than he did of his own immediate pleasure.

2

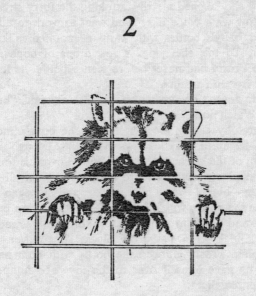

THE MORNING GARY brought the coon in I was late to work. But no matter. Few campers were up anyway, and only a handful of tourists had arrived and were walking among the redwoods. These would just have to look after themselves for an hour or two, I decided. First things first. Right at the moment, starting a tiny wild thing on the road through a strange new world seemed more urgent than anything else I could possibly do.

And where do you begin? Approximately where you'd start with a human baby--by feeding it. Since Assistant Ranger Mel Whittaker and his wife, Mary, had brought a new son home from the hospital the day before, I hurried to their house for advice.

As I expected, Mary knew how to help a little coon. "Oh!" she laughed merrily, stroking the furry stranger, "I know what *you'd* like," and went to work to fill one of her baby's bottles with warm evaporated milk and water. To this she added a few drops of honey. Because Frosty had never before seen a bottle, he leaned away from it fearfully.

"He doesn't know about bottles," Mary said, "but he will. Watch now."

Carefully easing the nipple into the coon's mouth, Mary began to work his jaws over it just enough that a stream of the warm, sweet milk flowed over his tongue. For a minute nothing more happened. Then all of a sudden—bingo! Frosty got the idea, and he began pulling on the nipple with all the energy of a suction pump. Mary and I had to wink at each other as we watched him. Quick as a flash, his black, shoe-button eyes gleaming, Frosty grabbed the bottle with both hands; then he gave himself over to the joys of whimpering with pure delight.

We let our baby take only a small portion of milk that first feeding, so he wouldn't founder. As the milk drained out of the bottle his flat belly began filling out. And as more and more milk vanished, his belly rounded so much that the white fur on it stood up, showing his hide, pink and clean.

Not being sure how much of Frosty's plumpness was milk and how much was air, I now turned him over my shoulder on a bath towel and started patting his behind. Sure enough, some of it was air. One whopping burp rumbled into the big outdoors.

"More room out than in," Mary laughed.

Relieved of his bubble, our little orphan soon became drowsy. Sleepily he put his head on my shoulder and closed his eyes. Almost at once peace spread over his flat, masked face like the benediction of a sunset on a storm-drenched landscape. Just before he slipped into coon dreamland, he laid a soft hand on my cheek and snuggled comfortably against my neck. With that, I became the only mother he would ever again know.

For most of an hour, while the park was swarming with visitors, I sat rocking my sleeping coon and talking about his future. "Somehow," I told Mary, "I'm going to have to figure out how to do my job and raise this little fellow at the same time."

You see, the members of a ranger crew have to put in as long a day as is necessary to maintain and operate their park efficiently. During the summer our days rarely ended with just eight hours. They had a way of going on and on into the night. Not only that, but we were on call around the clock. Like the others of the crew, I went to work soon after seven in the morning, and often didn't turn in until past midnight. But if things broke right I usually could manage a rest period after lunch.

Somehow, in such a schedule as this, I was going to have to make sure that Frosty got his bottle, and was burped, every two hours or so; that he had time to play out of doors; that he lived as happy a life as possible. It was a big order considering my chores in this huge state park.

I had to work at Headquarters part of the day; take out nature hikes; be at the Museum a couple of hours; walk through camp and picnic areas to welcome and inform our visitors (we had almost 300 campsites and half as many picnic tables, located in different directions from Park Center); plan and conduct the evening campfires, where hundreds of people gathered from seven o'clock until ten or so; and be around the Center afterwards for as long as seemed best. Providing we had no accidents, fires, lost campers, or other disasters, that generally was my day. Caring for little Frosty's needs was to punctuate this schedule at regular intervals from dawn until the wee small hours. Don't ask me how all of this got done, but it did. With the help of Park Naturalist Don Meadows, several other ranger neighbors, and a camper or two, Frosty did get his bottle and a burping on time for the next three weeks. With such devoted care as this, his frail body fattened. And something else: his coon wits sharpened to a needle-fine point. I discovered that one day.

By then I'd made my first mistake. In my eagerness to give our coon baby a good home, I let him see how cute I thought he was, and how much I loved him. But how could I have done otherwise? He was so tiny and darling; so soft and cuddly, so dependent. Still, I should have paid more attention to the way he studied my face from behind the nipple of his bottle. If I had, maybe I could have figured out what he was up to. Believe me, I'd know that look on any face now. I'd recognize it as being keenly alert and intelligent—and calculating. You might say it was similar to the look on the face of a boy who, while appearing to be deep in thought about his homework, had his snake collection slithering around in his lap.

The day came when Frosty's black eyes began to shine as if they had been polished. All of a sudden it hit me—what he was thinking—and it was plain as day: "Boy, is she a softie! She thinks I'm cute. This is going to be easy."

Believe it or not, it was. I fell for his tricks, and when I came to, it was too late. By then, he had everything under control.

It all began when he started taking his time about feeding. He'd pull on that nipple like mad for awhile, then he'd begin pat-a-caking his hands and sticking first one foot and then the other into his mouth. When I moved to take his bottle away, he'd grab it out of my hands and start working on it again. Couldn't I see that he wasn't finished with it yet?

This sort of thing could have gone on by the hour, for Frosty knew that when he had finished his bottle I would leave the house and go back on the job. And how he hated to be left alone with no one to make a fuss over him.

When at last I did walk out the front door, he could be heard halfway to Headquarters, screeching at the top of his lungs. Tourists from all over the world who had come to view the famous giant redwoods left the trees and came on a dead run. Wild-eyed, they hurried to find out what horrible thing was going on in that ranger residence. Within minutes, both of my porches filled with agitated people.

Every day these good folk left a fresh layer of noseprints on my window panes. None of them doubted for a minute that someone in my cabin was dying in agony. Naturally there were always some who ran to Headquarters to get help. In time, the already over-worked rangers got touchy and began to take a dim view of spoiled raccoons.

It was different with Frosty. After he once looked up and saw all those faces peering in at him, he decided he must be one Mighty Big Shot. From that moment on, he worked every angle.

As soon as word got around the park that I was raising a baby coon, my cabin became as congested as Disneyland on a holiday. Just about everyone from San Francisco south found his way to my door. "We hear you have a little coon," they'd say hopefully, with a certain upturn in their voices. And then they'd add, "could we please see him?"

Of course they could. I let them in even though I

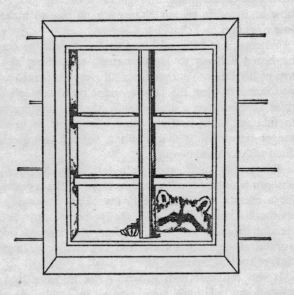

might have been trying my best to eat supper before it got stone cold or working on my Weekly Report or ironing a fresh uniform shirt to wear to campfire. Such things as these had to be pushed into the background, for someone was always coming into or going out of my cabin. Many days, my house wasn't big enough to hold all of Frosty's admirers.

The rangers laughingly called Ranger Residence No. 1 the Museum Annex, since they said it held the park's only live specimen. All the rest were mounted and in the display cases. Fortunately, the crew didn't tell Frosty about this or that he shared the spotlight with the greatest trees on earth. Heaven help us if they had! Managing him after that would have been too much for just one lady ranger.

Some of the visitors who called on Frosty had low, calm voices. Most of these were men and boys. With them he was mannerly and subdued—especially with the two Stanford zoology professors who came to see how he was put together. "Look," one of them said to the other as he examined the soles of Frosty's feet. "Plantigrade."

Education that high seemed to awe Frosty completely, and hobnobbing with Ph.D.'s proved to be too much for his usual aplomb. Even though the learned visitors explained that "plantigrade" meant walking on the feet the way man does—heel to toe—he still sat quietly in their laps, studying their faces so intently that I half expected them to lapse into a hypnotic trance. But all the time his nimble fingers were busy; not once did he stop exploring the professors' pockets, pulling their zippers up and down, and reaching inside their shirt fronts as far as he could. The whole time they were there, he felt around over their stomachs and chests. How he loved the smooth softness of the hide on these humans. Too bad they were so ticklish.

Most of Frosty's admirers were women, and there was rarely anything calm about them. They usually worked themselves into such a giggling, squealing tizzy over him that their already high-pitched voices shot into orbit. So then did Frosty. Like a commando scaling a cliff, he'd scramble up their bosoms to their shoulders, and sometimes even to the tops of their heads where he lost no time fingering their hair-do's all out of style. Then he'd always wind up by ramming an arm down inside the fronts of their dresses. You can imagine what such antics did to the dignity of our female visitors.

But what made Frosty really happy was to grab purses and dump their contents onto the floor. With much clatter, the most fascinating things always tumbled out and rolled around all over the place. The more loudly the women shrieked at this, the greater Frosty's zest. And Heaven help anyone who got down on the floor to retrieve her possessions. She only found herself involved in a game that was actually a contest to see whether Frosty could snatch all of her belongings away from her faster than she could pick them up. On such occasions as these, my cabin became a whirlpool of commotion in no time at all.

One day some Southern California friends, Nina and Dick, dropped in. They had no idea, of course, that anyone lived there besides me. So they sat down and made themselves at home while we chatted happily about their vacation travels. In the excitement I didn't quite get around to telling them about Frosty.

Meanwhile he was hiding in the bathroom, peeking out at them. That was his way. He rarely accepted people without first looking them over. If, after a short preliminary scrutiny, he decided they were all right (as he nearly always did), he then went all out to welcome them—suddenly, completely, and violently. No halfway stuff.

I believe we were discussing the accommodations at the Lodge when, unknowingly, my guests passed their probation period. With jet-propelled hospitality, and a dull thud, Frosty bounded out of the bathroom and landed on Dick's chest. As Dick, dumbfounded, grunted under the impact and recoiled from this hurtling object, he jerked away too far. He went right over backwards, chair and all. Riding him clear down to the floor was Frosty. Even before Dick could recover sufficiently to move, Frosty had snatched the pack of cigarettes out of his shirt pocket and was rolling some of them between his hands. This was only the beginning of a mania for the feel of cigarettes. After that, there was no one he wouldn't tackle to get at them.

Poor Dick. He never quite recovered from that crashing experience. In the years that followed, he and Nina were mighty careful to find out who else might be in my house before opening the screen door. I guess Dick wasn't used to landing on his back on the floor with his feet in the air and a raccoon clinging to his chest.

The trouble with having visitors in our cabin was that long after they had left Frosty was still grandstanding like the pampered halfback of some high school varsity. Talk about plain, pure ham! At first I thought all of this was terribly funny. He saw that I did, too, which inspired him to greater and greater heights. What I should have said was: "Now today's game is over; the crowd has gone home; off to the showers with you." But I didn't; and what a mistake that was! Twelve to sixteen hours' work a day, with vaudeville thrown in to fill up the rest of the time, was beginning to wear my sense of humor thin.

One busy Saturday night it wore clear through.

That was the day we had 15,000 people in the park; all campsites were filled; the Picnic Area was crowded to overflowing. During the morning two small barefoot boys wandered off into the forest. A motorist tried to see the tops of some 300-foot redwoods while rounding a sharp turn. A woman teased a deer she shouldn't have been feeding. By early afternoon the entire ranger crew was on duty, and not one of us could find time to eat any lunch. Added to all this was the yellow kitten that Darrell Knoeffler, one of the rangers, had found stalking a chipmunk and brought to Headquarters. Since I had volunteered to find homes for any cats that strayed into the park and developed an interest in our wildlife, Darrell deposited her on my desk.

"A little something to beef up your day," he quipped, giving my arm a friendly squeeze. I threw him a dirty look, but as always he grinned, touching the brim of his Stetson in mock salute. "Have fun," he added, and then swung briskly out the door. That was all I needed that day—a kitten.

Impatiently I turned my attention to our unwelcome guest. I had to admit that she was a darling little thing, even if she had chosen to explore Big Basin. Her eyes were big and blue, her fur short and plushy, the color of gold. She was just Frosty's size exactly. Never having introduced a coon and a kitten, I wondered what Frosty would do to her—or the other way around. Well, I decided, I'd better find out, for I had to take her over to my cabin. I went to the storeroom and got the animal carrying cage, put her into it, and headed for the house.

As soon as I put the cage on the floor and opened its door, out walked the little gold nugget, mewing plaintively. Stiff-legged, Frosty drew away, flattened his head against his shoulders, and laid his ears back. Neither had ever seen one of the other kind before.

While they eyed each other warily, I held my breath and waited.

For an electric moment both remained perfectly still. Then explosively, with all the delicate restraint of a cyclone, love burst into bloom. In an all-out rush that really should have scared the kitten half to death, Frosty bounded toward her with the Welcome Mat. Yet very gently he wrapped his arms around her neck— and hugged her. *Squish!* Before she could gather herself together to spit at him, her heart melted completely. Frosty made goo of everyone like that.

My gooey heart got harder than a rock before the next morning. But that afternoon when I left the house I was relaxed, and for once Frosty didn't screech me all the way to Headquarters. He was so busy it must have slipped his mind.

Already he had started swaggering and strutting back and forth, showing his guest what a terrific boy he was, and she was loving every minute of it. Everything he did made her eyes big with wonder. Of all the audiences he had so far played to, she made him feel the most important. Naturally he was going to live it up. As I closed the front door behind me I had to laugh, for I could hear Frosty's games of Hide-and-Seek and Tag romping noisily from the bathroom to the kitchen. I hoped Goldie was beginning to get the hang of how it all went.

"Well," I muttered aloud as I headed across Park Center, "maybe I'm going to live through this day after all."

That's what I thought—although all afternoon I had no cause to feel otherwise. Every time I looked in on Frosty and the kitten I saw that they were having fun. Happy with each other, they had even left their food untouched. Moreover, Frosty was so agog about showing off that he hardly noticed me at all. Every-thing seemed to be going fine.

So in the evening I went peacefully to conduct the campfire, and afterwards patroled for an hour or two in the pickup with one of the rangers.

Just before midnight I turned homeward at last, tired and ready for some rest. The next day would be Sunday, our big day of the week. Nearly all of us would be on the job from early until late, because Big Basin was sure to be jammed with even more tourists. As I walked down the path leading to my cabin, I remember thinking that I must be quiet, for Frosty and Goldie would be asleep. I even took off my boots so I could tiptoe into the house without disturbing them. "Don't stir up a rumpus at this hour," I cautioned myself.

As I eased the door open and peeked in, there was a resounding crash that echoed through the house and forest. A stack of kettles had tumbled off the low shelf under the sink, and with nerve-wracking clatter and din were rolling and rattling their separate ways all over the kitchen floor. By the time I got to them, Frosty had planted himself pertly in the middle of the biggest one, and was beaming at me. Nearby sat the kitten, wide-eyed with admiration.

"Oh, no!" I breathed, unbelieving. "You can't still be at it!"

Oh, yes, but he was, he told me unmistakably, with a quick toss of his head and eyes sparkling merrily. Yes, indeedy!

Blessed with an audience of two, now that I was home, Frosty shifted into high gear. Swaggering from room to room, he took a swipe at both wastebaskets, tipped them over, and began strewing their contents far and wide. I discovered that he had removed the laces from my shoes, too, and that he had hidden in various places every one of the twenty pounds or so of English walnuts that had been in the lug box beside the kitchen stove. For weeks they rolled out of chairs and closet corners, sometimes without warning in the middle of the night. In addition, Frosty had climbed the bedspread and made his way to the bedside table, where he helped himself to the contents of my jewel case. At the end of the summer I found bracelets, beads, and earrings tucked away in the bedsprings and under the bathtub.

Sagging with weariness, I stumbled into the bathroom, only to find that my coon had generously powdered the floor with the can of Borax. What a mess! I dragged myself into the kitchen, got my mop and bucket, and went to work to clean it up. It took me a long time, what with Frosty riding the mop back and forth the way he did. Afterwards he had fun blockprinting the walls with his wet hands as high as he could reach. Every few minutes he'd look over his shoulder at the kitten for approval, which he sure got, although somewhat numbly now. She was almost asleep with her eyes open, but she still thought he was wonderful. Filled with the joy of living, Frosty rose to bigger and finer things as the night—and I—dragged on.

By the time it appeared that I might go to bed at last, the kitten was swaying with exhaustion, her eyelids hanging at half mast. Once she fell over while trying to focus her eyes on her hero, who was just then trying to pull the bath mat out from under her.

At 1:30 A.M., bleary-eyed with fatigue after nineteen hours on the go, I filled Frosty's hot water bottle and put it into his box. Then, as always, I put him on it. "That," I thought, "is that for tonight."

But it wasn't. He simply climbed out and took up where he'd left off before I had so rudely interrupted him. Almost unable to navigate any longer, I dropped

into a chair in the living room and closed my eyes
while Frosty ran circles around the kitten trying to
make her dizzy. He kept at it, too, until she fell flat.
Taking a deep breath I said aloud, "This has to stop
now. You're a perfect little stinker!" Then I got up
and, for the first time, picked Frosty up and paddled
him.

You'd have thought such a surprising and shocking
thing as this would have stopped his shenanigans then
and there—but oh my, no. Frosty took it as applause
even if he did take it on his rear end. Smiling broadly
in appreciation, he hurried back to his cat-circling to
see if he could make Goldie fall over a second time.

For that I paddled him again. Still he persisted. I
grew desperate. I paddled him again and again, and
the paddlings got harder until I was ashamed. Yet my
disciplinary intent completely escaped my small coon.
Really fired up with so much approval, he went right
on, joyously cramming his normal waking hours (and
my sleeping ones) full of all those things that delighted
his little coon heart.

At 2:30 A.M. his daytime and my graveyard shift
met head on. "You're through for tonight, young man!
Finished! *Kaput!*" I bellowed. Shaking with anger and
frustration, I stuffed him and his hot water bottle into
the cat cage, and stomped out to the garage. There I
stowed the cage in the car, shut the car door, shut the
garage door, the house door, and the bedroom door. I
climbed into bed and pulled the covers over my ears.
Within minutes Big Basin was quiet at last, except for
the occasional bits of foliage that drifted down from
high places.

Next morning I gave the kitten a bowl of milk and
hurried to the garage, not knowing what I'd find.
"Surely," I mumbled to myself, "he's pulled the cage to
pieces by now and has unscrewed every nut and bolt

inside the car. I'll bet anything he has the dashboard clock in pieces on the floor." With Frosty anything could have happened.

But nothing had. Nothing whatever. There in his cage was the furry little angel, curled up in a tight ball, hands covering his face. Once he peeked furtively at me from between his fingers. Then, very, very slowly he turned away. Obviously he wanted me to think he was asleep.

Inside the house I lifted him out of the cage and put him into his box. There he huddled in one corner with his back to me. He even refused his bottle. Quite a change from the cocky brat of the night before!

"Okay," I said, "I'll be independent, too." So a great big silence filled the cabin. We ignored each other completely. He pouted in his corner; I ate breakfast without a word; and both of us were thoroughly miserable.

Every hour or two all morning I came home and offered Frosty his bottle. But he would have none of it. Instead, he continued to crouch in the corner of his box without as much as a glance in my direction.

At midmorning Goldie was adopted by an elderly woodcutter and his wife down the canyon a few miles. I hope the kitten finally recovered from being an all-night rooting section, and wasn't worn out the rest of her life. One thing sure: she was going to have a loving home; she'd find no three-ring circus going on there.

As these good people drove away with their new pet, I took one more look at Frosty. He was still huddled in one corner of his box. Not very happily I left the house and returned to headquarters, thinking to myself that with Frosty I had to carry through. It was now or never. We had to find out who was boss in our family.

At lunchtime it seemed that temporarily, at least, I

was. Or maybe hunger pangs drove Frosty to seek forgiveness. Anyway, when I sat down to eat, he crawled slowly and reluctantly out of his box and, head down, ambled over to my chair and leaned against my foot. After a minute or two I gently picked him up.

Naturally I thought his first interest would be his bottle, but it wasn't. Instead, he climbed my jacket front and snuggled under my chin. Then he pressed his cold nose against my throat, and slipped an arm around my neck. More important to him than food, just at that moment, was telling me he was sorry, and that he wanted to make up so he could feel the warmth of my love once more. "You little scamp," I murmured softly, responding to his need by holding him against me gently and securely.

I know that he understood. No words were really necessary; but they broke a long, unwanted silence, and they must have been as comforting to him as his answering trill was to me. It came out of him querulously. At first it was almost inaudible, but it grew stronger and stronger as I patted him reassuringly. Pretty soon it became a mighty outpouring of pent-up grief.

Now who would have a heart so hard it couldn't melt when a baby coon confesses he has been a stinker, and promises not to do such things again—until he finds another opportunity? Not I. But I did tell him he'd better be more considerate of me, or I wouldn't last long enough to help him grow up and be free.

Shyly he finally brought himself to look up at me. A bottle of warm milk and honey convinced him that regardless of yesterday's flunk in deportment, he was beloved just the same.

And so ended my first lesson on how to discipline a sweet little coon. I had found that you could spank him till your hands were sore, and never change his mind one iota. But if you hurt his feelings he would fall apart, then and there. *Anything* but the horror of being banished to solitary confinement, with no audience to play to or anyone to love you!

3

RESTORED TO FULL flower, Frosty's heart once more began to bubble over. He put his creative spirit to work by inventing all kinds of ways to entertain himself when he was alone during my work hours. For one thing, he'd play endlessly with the blue jay feathers I'd bring home from my walks through the park. Eagerly grabbing them out of my hand, he'd toss them in the air until they were too ragged to be interesting any longer. The rest of the time he'd sleep or prowl the house, stalk the hot water tank or finger the string of keys the rangers were collecting for him. And how he loved to paddle in his pan of water with its celluloid ducks.

Many times during the day he climbed the bed-spread and crawled into the open window. There he'd sit looking out through the screen at the half dozen or more deer who would be standing outside the cabin, waiting for a handout. They were wonderful company; Frosty talked companionably with them by the hour. Many days I found him visiting, instead, with a group of fascinated tourists. He would chirr and trill at them as long as they stayed to exclaim over him. With so many people passing my house, as they walked among the giant redwoods, he had little time to be lonesome.

My problem was making sure he had enough rest. After all, he was still a baby, and would have slept a lot had he been with his mother in the family den. It is Nature's way that her coons sleep most of the day, and then prowl at night. Any time after dusk you can expect to see park coons. Yet, for the season, I had to turn Frosty's days and nights around. I just couldn't stay awake the full twenty-four hours.

From the start he seemed willing to accept my way of life. Late in the evening, after I had come home for the night, we'd have a snack and play for a while. Then, when I was ready for bed, I would help him climb into his box. Before I could turn out the light, he'd be curled up in a ball on his hot water bottle—fast asleep.

About daybreak, when Big Basin grew quite cold, Frosty always climbed out of his box, came to my bed, and whimpered to be taken in with me. Barely awake, he'd seek my shoulder to lay his head upon, and be lost in dreams almost immediately. He was the best of snugglers. Together we'd settle down in cozy compan-ionship for another hour of sleep. Never once did I have reason to feel that he wasn't clean enough to share my bed.

For the rest of the summer this was the way we were to manage. "When Labor Day comes," I told him, "we'll see what to do next. I've been asked to stay on here after Labor Day this year, and since I can write in my off-duty hours, we may do just that."

Following that last big holiday of the season, most vacationers went home, leaving Big Basin empty and quiet. From then on through the autumn, until the winter rains came in October or November, nearly all the park visitors would be weekend picnickers and tourists. I decided we could figure out more about how to prepare Frosty for his future at that time. Meanwhile we had other problems.

Because it couldn't possibly be right for this Big Basin coon not to feel the rough, deeply-furrowed bark of his redwood trees, or know the wet mysteries of all the park creeks, I gave him most of my off-duty time. Some days we played Hide-and-Seek in and out a big, old, fire-hollowed redwood back of the park maintenance shops. The great, blackened cave in its base was large enough to hold two dozen people—although it seldom did, because few knew it was there. Once in a while a family or a small group of hikers would discover it. Visitors liked to turn their flashlight beams upward, just to see how tall that room-in-a-tree was. Their torches usually weren't powerful enough to reach so far, but they did find the bats that were clinging to the blackened walls high up in the burn.

Typical of most fire-ravaged redwoods, this one was healing its injury. Long ago it had started putting out new, woody "flesh" all around the edges of the burn, in much the same manner that our bodies manufacture scar tissue. One day the giant would close its gaping wound entirely. Generations hence, tourists gazing up

in wonder at the tree's enormous bulk wouldn't know that inside was a blackened cavity. Only after the giant fell would the true story of its long survival be revealed.

But this would probably be centuries hence—many centuries. Frosty and I, with our mere instant on earth, weren't concerned with such things. We enjoyed the big old tree because here he could romp in the sun among the rolling surface roots; here he could secrete himself in the dark recess of the giant's burned-out interior, and then come bounding out to wrestle with me. We came often.

Other days, when few campers were in the lower campground, we'd take our hour or two after lunch and follow Union Creek. Along its banks Frosty would play with the waxy spears of trillium and rustle around in the miner's lettuce and alum root for all sorts of things that wriggled and squirmed. And when he tired of this, he'd hide among the huckleberry bushes and, eyes aglow, leap out at me. The more he thought he scared me, the more he enjoyed his little game.

Then there were days when we'd take a ride to Sky Meadow to see if we could find any mountain iris left over from May and June; or we'd go up to where Sempervirens Falls spills over its sandstone cliff, and hunt in the shade there for star flowers. We never picked them, of course. We just looked at them. In our public preserves you leave things where they are for other people to see. And that goes for rangers and coons as well as visitors.

We couldn't get away every afternoon. State and national parks teem with people in the summer. There is much to do for them, and things happen. In countless parks, ranger crews remain on a schedule of unlimited hours throughout the season. Sometimes we at Big Basin had to stand by on our days off. Many an afternoon Frosty and I got no farther away from our cabin than the crater—less than a dozen yards from the front porch. But even so, we had fun.

This crater, like all the others you find in a coastal redwood forest, has nothing whatever to do with any kind of volcanism. Rather, it is a bowl-shaped depression in the ground, left by huge roots that have wrenched free of the earth and upended when a giant tree toppled over.

A fallen redwood can leave quite a hole. It isn't deep, for the giant tree's root system is surprisingly shallow, but it is often twenty feet or so in diameter. In time it becomes smooth and rounded and soft with duff. And it is a wonderfully secluded place because of the young redwoods standing close together around the perimeter.

Perhaps a dozen or more centuries ago these same redwoods were little ones, rising out of the surface roots of the mother tree. There were more of them then, but the others withered and died in brutal competition for sunlight while they were still fuzzy saplings. Those that now form a living ring around a crater are the hardy ones, many of them fully mature and giants in their own right. No two of their diameters or heights are the same. They run two, four, six feet across—even eight and ten.

These craters are a great delight to campers. As one man said, "We're from the Midwest. In Kansas everything's flat and one big, wide-open space. We just can't believe that our *whole* camp- -tent, picnic table, food locker, and stone stove—can *all* fit down inside a ring of enormous trees, and with room to spare."

The crater beside my cabin wasn't that big, but it was cozy. Along about one o'clock in the afternoon the sun shone down into it for almost half an hour. Out there Frosty and I could be in the open, at home, and still not actually in our home, all at the same time.

Within that ring of redwoods we could escape briefly from park visitors who were unable to read signs, and who, therefore, would come knocking on our door to ask their way to the Picnic Area or the Chimney Tree. Frosty loved the crater. He scratched in the duff for bugs, and never seemed to tire of fingering the new, foot-high redwoods that were stump-sprouting abundantly around the larger ones of the circle.

I tried to read, but that was often a lost cause. Frosty was too interested in the toeless slippers I wore during my relaxing time. The holes fascinated him. I think he always expected something to pop out of them. Every few minutes he'd reach into one—or both and feel my toes, all the while gazing up into the treetops with a vacant expression on his face, the way coons do. It was as if no connection existed between his thoughts and his busywork. But it did, anyway. His brain was directing those talented hands; it knew exactly what they were doing.

The afternoon Frosty poked his black-knobbed nose into the hole of one of my shoes and nipped my big toe, ended that activity. In order to satisfy his curiosity and read my book in peace, I took off the shoe and gave it to him. But that logical little plan went awry. Frosty merely deserted the shoe, climbed onto my shoulders, straddled the back of my neck, and sat there mussing my hair while I struggled on and on, determined to find out how the story ended.

Frosty liked to ride on my shoulders on some of the hikes, too—a leg dangling around each side of my neck, hands gripping my hair for dear life. Once, by riding a part of the distance, he went a mile and a half down the Waddell Canyon with me. This trek we had to save for one of my days off, because the trail required time and patience. You couldn't walk along on it as on all the others in the park. It was extremely narrow, and parts had already collapsed into the creek. Today it is all gone.

That day we started early and took our time. There were so many things to see; so many birdcalls to hear. The air was dank and musty, although clean and fresh, too, as fog would seem exquisitely clean and fresh to anyone coming out of a stuffy, overheated house. Even at midday the shade down in there was dense. Largely because of it, moss and ferns—especially sword ferns—covered all the fallen monarchs with a blanket of living green.

We had our lunch on a tiny sandbar beside one of those stands of giant woodwardias you find down the Waddell. Frosty had a big time hiding among them and peeking out at me. To him these ferns were a towering, altogether friendly forest. They were more his size than the massive redwoods rising skyward all around us. He didn't care much for them, although he liked to climb over their surface roots, providing I was there with him. On several occasions he had found himself alone on the far side of one of these behemoths. Suddenly he was completely cut off from everything familiar. He couldn't see me anywhere, and he panicked. To Frosty, a redwood was just too much tree.

After we ate our lunch we crawled out onto a huge boulder. Since it was a flattish slab, I stretched out comfortably to rest and listen to the sweet song of a thrush, soaring above the gurglings of the water. While I relaxed, Frosty decided to investigate some potholes in the rock, left after white water had torn small boulders from their conglomerate matrix, and then swirled them round and round in place for perhaps centuries before carrying them away. As stony foxholes for a little coon to play in, they were a perfect fit. Happily he ran from one to the other, patting the circular smoothness of each with his hands.

Later we picked our way still farther downcanyon, stopping often so that Frosty could lose himself in glades of bracken and study his reflection in quiet pools. Several times he tried to touch the coon he saw in the water, but somehow he could never manage it. This puzzled him.

To divert his attention from the problem, I almost pointed out the wet moss of a water ouzel's nest that was tucked in among the rocks near a waterfall not far away. But I didn't. Its occupants were minding their own business. They were diving into the deeper water and walking along the sandy bottom in search of larvae and such as casually as if they were strolling on dry ground. One of the oddities among feathered folk are these that bob at the knees every second; they can jump into a rushing creek and be carried downstream on a watery rollercoaster, climb out, and do it all over again—just for the joy of it. I should not have let a little coon bother them, although he might have helped them find what they were looking for on the streambed.

So we went on down below the waterfall, and thinking to add to his store of knowledge, I showed him the only nutmeg tree in the park. But it impressed him not one bit—especially after he spotted the scouring rushes (or horsetails) on the other side of some marsh shallows. Still feeling that I should inform him further about his wilderness, I called, "Know something? Back in prehistoric times the rushes you're playing in were as big as the redwoods. Why do you suppose Our Father chose to keep the big trees as they were, and reduce these lovely things to mere dwarfs?"

Frosty paid no attention whatever to my efforts in his behalf; he was in no mood for philosophy. By then he had found a banana slug crawling along the top of a rotting log, and was remodeling it.

Because of my busy schedule, most of the jaunts

Frosty and I took had to be much shorter than the trek down the Waddell Canyon. On those days, when time crowded us into an hour or less for our recreation, we'd steal away from Park Center and drive a couple of miles up an old park maintenance road, used only by the rangers. There, in a certain clump of redwoods and firs, we'd leave the car and follow a short trail down to Opal Creek. Frosty always bobbed along at my heels like a puppy until he heard the water playing softly over the rocks. Then, with a cry of gladness, he'd scamper on ahead and jump in. To him, everything was an exciting adventure.

Times to remember were these we had to ourselves, far from the throngs of vacationers. While Frosty felt around in the riffles for crayfish and other creatures a coon likes to catch, I'd sit nearby, among the shamrock leaves of the oxalis, lean back against a tree, and watch. He'd trill contentedly, and I'd answer in my own way so that between ourselves we had a very satisfying conversation. The only other sounds we heard were the songs of birds and the bubbling of Opal Creek as it moved downslope toward the Waddell, thence to the mecca of all western waters—the Pacific Ocean, seventeen miles away.

Our giant forest was companionable. On warm, dry days, patches of sun drew a pleasing aroma from the thick carpet of redwood needles underfoot; on cool, foggy days, the streamside ferns glistened with a million diamonds just waiting to be shaken into spray by little coon hands; in June and early July, the air was filled with the sweet fragrance of the creamy-white azaleas that hung in masses over the creeks, and were mirrored in their glassy pools; during August, loaded huckleberry bushes invited us to harvest their fruit, which we often did.

Watching Frosty's pleasure at the creek was a real

tonic for me. For one thing, I, too, am a worshipper of
mountain streams. For another, it was something we
shared. I've always thought that people, with all their
luxury gadgets, take far too many simple things for
granted—things like being able to splash around in
clear, running water. But then I would think that way—
I who had lived so many years in Southern California,
where for a few days a creekbed can be a muddy
torrent, and the rest of the year a dusty, desolate pile
of boulders.

So I felt as Frosty did about Opal Creek, except that
I didn't have quite the same need of it that he had. My
need was mostly aesthetic. His was because Nature had
constructed him and all his kind to be dependent upon
water, not only for food supply and refuge from enemies, but for the greatest enjoyment of life. The water
could be the noisy swirls at the bottom of a canyon, or
the ripples that lap the shores of lakes and reservoirs,
or the quiet mirrors of marshes, ponds, and lagoons. It
could be the tidepools among the rocks along the edge
of the sea or the waves rushing up on a beach and
back down again. It could be the fountains and leaky
faucets and birdbaths in people's yards. But water in
some form a coon must have; and water he will get to.
Never will he be very far from it.

At first I expected Frosty to wash all his food if
water were handy—as it usually was, of course. But he
didn't. He just washed it occasionally, when he felt a
real need, or was in a mood to eat and play with water
at the same time. I soon discovered, though, that the
inside of a coon's mouth is quite dry—not only Frosty's,
but that of every coon I have fed. They seem to
have little saliva. So I wouldn't be surprised if they
don't dunk, instead of wash, their food so it will go
down more easily—the way we do with our doughnuts
and coffee.

To each of our afternoon outings I always brought refreshments that Frosty could dip in the stream if he wanted to. We relished them out there among the ferns and oxalis much more than we did at home in the cabin. When I'd open my paper sack and hold out a piece of cake or a bunch of grapes to Frosty, his black eyes would shine and his mouth open in a big, winsome smile. Then he'd come on the gallop, dripping all the way, and trilling in his anticipation and delight.

What more than all this could we have wanted?

Yet many times I wondered if Frosty did wish for more—his complete freedom. I also wondered what he would do with it if he had it; if I weren't there to look after his every want. Would he just naturally wander away perhaps, and disappear into the wilderness? Would some coon mother take him into her brood, and raise him as her own? Some way I had to find out.

One afternoon, while we were at our favorite spot on Opal Creek, I decided fearfully that this was the day. I might lose Frosty, but I had to know. Aloud I said, "Dear Father of both of us, if it's good for this little thing to go back to his own now, please guide his footsteps. Above all, Father, please keep him safe. We will do what You decide is right."

Heart pounding, I stepped behind a big old redwood and waited.

For moments that seemed to stretch into hours, I could hear only the bubbling of the creek and my own breathing. Leaning back against the great giant that had begun life here before the time of Christ, I grew more and more tense as the minutes passed.

Then I heard it—the trilling I had come to know so well. Frosty was splashing out of the creek and calling, not happily and lightly as he always had, but excitedly. Like wind sweeping across the plains his voice rose to a wail; his cries poured out, tumbling pell-mell over each other. At first they were in bewilderment and fright. Then very fast they changed to piercing shrieks of terror as he rushed this way and that, searching for me. I had never before witnessed such panic—even in my own kind.

This was all I needed. Quickly stepping out from behind the tree, I dropped onto the ground. Frosty saw me and, with one long quavering screech of relief, came bounding as fast as his legs could carry him. Soaking wet, he climbed my front, wrapped his arms around my neck, and clung with all the strength of his desperation. I had my answer.

For a long time I sat there, gently patting him and trying to help him feel secure again. And when he had calmed down at last, I dried both of us with his towel and said, "Now, little one, until you *want* to leave, I will take care of you the best I know how. We have just been told that I am your family, and you are mine. Come on. Let's go home and have our bottles."

We did. He had milk and honey and a dash of orange juice; I had a coke with a dash of lemon. And there was a strong, new bond between us. For better or for worse, we would be together until the wilds would call him back.

What a time in our lives that was going to be!

4

IN ADDITION TO an hour or more most afternoons, I also had Mondays off—*if* there were no emergency that necessitated my remaining on duty. The weekend rushes were over by then; many of the campers had left for home or for visits to others of California's scenic spots; the park had its day of quiet, and so did I.

About Wednesday our campgrounds would begin to fill up again, and by Friday afternoon Big Basin would once more teem with people; by Saturday evening, activity would have reached fever pitch—all campsites taken, all Lodge cabins spoken for. By Sunday night I would again be ready for a nice, restful Monday. And so it went, week after week, all summer, every summer, year in and year out for the twenty summers that I was in the California State Park Service. This was the way each member of the crew, on his one precious day off had to do his personal things and get some relaxing, too.

Frosty and I usually drove 25 miles down the San Lorenzo Canyon to Santa Cruz for supplies. He liked to take this ride as he had his "hike" down the Waddell—by sitting astride the back of my neck, holding onto my hair and ears. Once in a while he chose to sit upon the steering wheel crossbars, legs hanging over, and grip the rim; so that, in a manner of speaking, he was helping to steer the car. But too many oncoming motorists saw him as they approached and passed, and so many of them, in their amazement, narrowly missed the next curve, that we finally decided to use only country roads after that for our dual-control driving.

On the days when there were only a few errands to attend to, we could spend most of the time having fun. Then we'd visit with the ranger families and their pets in the state parks along Monterey Bay, occasionally down-coast as far as Big Sur. Other Mondays we'd picnic out in the forest beside a stream or pond. We even explored along the edge of the sea.

Frosty loved to get excited about the little creatures the ebbing tide left behind. On the shoreline rocks, among the long, thin blades of the eel grass, he found all sorts of things. There were limpets by the score, and there were small crabs that challenged his ingenuity because, unless he handled them just so, they pinched him with their claws. Yet he seemed to enjoy trying to outwit them. Try as he would, though, he could never pull the miniature sea tangle off the rocks, or the feathery rock kelp, either. Their holdfasts held too fast for him. The barnacles and black mussels, inactive at low tide, he couldn't get to move at all.

Most especially Frosty loved the tidepools. They were so alive when the tide was out. Down among the sea urchins and the glossy red and purple sea silk and the bunches of sea fingers lived many marine characters that had to scoot swiftly to escape little coon hands. There were, for instance, cone shells and black turbans; they scurried around, propelled by legs not their own, but belonging instead to those tidepool clowns, the hermit crabs, who move into any empty shell that happens to fit.

A Monday or two Frosty turned up a starfish down in the tidepools and—another Monday, in a dark watery crevice, one of those small octopi that live near the shore. This squirmy monstrosity, with its tenacious eight-way stretch, Frosty soon found he could do without—if he could ever get rid of it. You'd think such things as this would have made him cautious. On the contrary, they only served to whet his curiosity. In seconds he'd be fishing around again for the slow and unwary in the same cold, crystal-clear pool among the seaside rocks.

"This is the life," I said, watching a sea anemone close up on the finger Frosty had poked into his mouth. He didn't answer. He was too busy, his hands exploring the submarine garden, his eyes intent on the beach nearby—on three avocets strolling into the lacy foam just then sliding upsand from the first line of breakers.

Something about the avocets must have intrigued him, for a moment later he headed their way on the double. Naturally, no birds are going to stay around to be examined minutely by any coon. But that didn't seem to disappoint Frosty. When the avocets abandoned ship, he promptly turned his attention else-

where—to the kelp the surf had cast up on the sand
and left there in great, stringy heaps. These were just
the thing for little coon hands because they were still
wet and slippery, their leathery blades twisted and
entwined with the bulbs and long, snake-like stems.
Panting with delight, Frosty rummaged through one of
the piles, which immediately stirred up a cloud of
sandhoppers and set a colony of fiddler crabs digging
frantically into the wet sand. Then, like a Wall Street
broker reading his ticker tape, he went over every foot
of the seaweed, inch by inch.

Most of our Mondays were like this—full of variety
and adventure, for Frosty threw himself into his trea-
sure hunts with gay abandon. He reached and he
fingered and he excavated. He dug up and tried to
chew the flat sand-dollar shells; he patted the chunks
of nearly transparent, blue-white jellyfish lying on the
sand near high-tide line; he galloped from dry beach
down to wet, chasing the backwash into the next front
of churning foam; then he turned and galloped up the
shining sand, making perfect little hand and foot prints
for the inrushing sea to erase almost as fast as he left
them.

Nearly all the pocket beaches along the north coast-
line above Santa Cruz are covered with shells of every
size and shape, and in numbers to defy the imagina-
tion. Among them, and also of every size and shape,
are pretty, flat rocks that have been tumbled and rolled
smooth by salt water for centuries on end. A whole
host of critters, both animal and vegetable, live there in
this intertidal zone—critters that have been able to
adapt themselves to the in-and-out movement of the
water. It is probably one of the most populous areas on
earth. I didn't know the name of everything I saw, and
I didn't particularly care. Frosty and I just enjoyed
them, every one.

How exhilarating were these days along the ocean, and how startlingly blue! After a week in the deep shade down on the floor of the world's tallest forest, it was thrilling, indeed, to see far horizons and fill my lungs with salt air. I could turn toward an onshore breeze so that my hair would blow back off my face, and look all I wanted to at the vastness of sunshine and sky and water spread out before me. I could glory in the fine salt spray that peppered my skin. Certainly I could never feel hemmed in, as I sometimes did at Big Basin by Sunday night. For a few heavenly hours I could be a spirit liberated. I could identify with the gulls I saw wheeling and soaring above the blue-green swells that rose and fell, rose and fell, rose and fell, just as they had been doing since the world began.

But by late afternoon most Mondays, both Frosty and I would again be ready to return to our forest primeval. We would be weary of so much space, so much blue, the glare of so much water; the rhythmic, never-ending roar of the breakers as they crashed down upon the beach and shattered themselves against the rocky shoreline.

We would now find the deepening shadows and dim light of our redwood realm soft and peaceful and satisfying beyond words. By the time we were well upcanyon toward Big Basin, the sun's last rays would be filtering down through the trees in long, slanting shafts. Everywhere would be the hush of eventide—the benediction on a day that had been beautiful to see, and happily lived.

By then the wild exhilaration of the seashore would have spent itself. I would be rested and refreshed. Orangey lights, shining out of mountain cabin windows here and there along the way, would look cozy and inviting. The majestic trees, no longer too big and too overpowering, would seem, once again, to be friends and family, and to be welcoming us home.

Long before we could ever reach Boulder Creek, and turn off to Big Basin, Frosty would be sound asleep in my lap—limp, worn out, caring nothing now for the likes of seaweed and avocets; no longer the Terror of the Tidepools.

"You've had quite a day, little man," I'd say aloud. "You'll soon be ready for bed, and so will I." The thought made me yawn.

Rounding turn after turn down into the park from the Summit, I noticed with pleasure that the cool of approaching night was soothing my sun-reddened face. Aromas of hot coffee and barbecuing meat, well seasoned, hung in the smoke of many campfires. Only one or two people stood at the Information window of Park Headquarters as I drove past. A few more watched the half dozen or so deer that had lain down in the rushes of the cienega in Park Center. What an utterly peaceful sight, I thought. What a relaxed day we've had.

But not all our Mondays were like this one.

One particular Monday, near the end of summer, stands out in my memory, far above the rest.

The day started out like all the others. We drove down to Santa Cruz, pulled into the parking lot of a supermarket, and I strolled in with my grocery list. But this morning I neglected to check my glove compartment first. That was something I should have remembered to do, too, for Frosty was now big enough that, by stretching, he could just reach the compartment from the car seat. He had already found that I kept all kinds of things in it that he could twist, rip, pull apart, jingle, and juggle. I *would* have to forget those medicated throat discs I'd tossed in there on our way down!

If you have ever taken one of these things you know

that you have to keep it moving around with your tongue or soon you begin to feel like an active volcano. You're half afraid to open your mouth for fear flames will shoot out. Frosty didn't know all of this, of course, and nothing would have changed his mind if he had.

As soon as I disappeared into the market, he began to figure ways of entertaining himself. As anyone might expect, he pulled open the glove compartment and seized the little box he saw in there. Here was something new! Frosty was always fascinated with new things. So he opened the box, and into his mouth popped not one, but a whole handful of those throat discs. With this he became the only known coon fire-eater.

I was busy investigating some bargains on the market shelves when I began to hear all the shouting. Wild-eyed people started running up and down the aisles calling loudly, "Who owns the Plymouth with the raccoon in it? Who owns the coon in the blue Plymouth?"

"I do," I called with a cold feeling of foreboding in the pit of my stomach.

"You'd better hurry up!" a man shouted breathlessly from the breakfast food section as more people crowded in beside him.

"What's wrong?" I asked.

"Your coon's gone mad," one of the women wailed hysterically.

"He's frothing at the mouth," a boy yelled, waving his arms.

"Rabies!"

"Nothing but rabies!"

"It's horrible!"

"We'll have to call the police!"

"He'll have to be shot. That's all you can do."

That did it. You bet there was something I could do.

Suddenly, what had happened struck me with the force
of a sledgehammer. Realizing full well, I tore for the
nearest exit to the parking lot.

On the way I streaked past the icebox full of milk
and soft drinks. Almost turning a flip in order to double
back, I managed to snatch a bottle of Seven Up, yank
it into the wall bottle opener, and rush out the door
ahead of the crowd. I had never moved so fast in all
my life.

Almost everything they had said was true. Frosty
was screeching and frothing and nearly mad with pain
and fear. He was ricocheting all over the car. Unlock-
ing the door, I jumped in, grabbed my coon, and held
him to me with all the strength I could muster. It
wasn't hard, though, to get the bottle of Seven Up in
his hot little mouth. He was willing—mighty willing.
The way he gulped that cooling liquid, you'd have
thought he had just dragged himself across the scorch-
ing sands of Death Valley.

As the drink cooled off his inner sanctum, his
screams gave way to small whimpers of relief. And by
the time he'd consumed half the fizz, his hands were
working on the bottle as they had on his bottle at
home, when he was filling up with milk and honey, and
was about to fall asleep.

I began to get my hair back down on my head.
Rolling the window down I spoke to all the folk who
had gathered round, and were staring in at us. "Well,"
I remarked, "this is the closest I've ever come to single-
handedly answering a three-alarm fire. But everything's
under control now."

It was. But only for a moment.

Just then a flatbed truck, loaded with wire cages of
loudly cackling and clucking hens, pulled in beside us.
I hardly noticed them, but, believe me, Frosty did.

Instinctively, I suppose, he knew what that racket was. He raised up and looked out over the heads of his amazed public. At the sight of so many feathers all together in one place, he lighted up like a Worlds Fair. Here were not a few measly feathers to play with, but thousands and thousands and *thousands!*

Before I could collect any of my wits, Frosty was climbing out the window. Using the shoulders, faces, and heads of the onlookers as a living bridge, he scrambled aboard the truck and up the stack of crates to the summit. Trilling and squealing with unbounded delight—and grinning his head off—he thumped and bounced up and down on one cage after another.

Well now, how do you describe a scene like this one with mere words? All I can say is that terrified people scattered in all directions. In the next instant, at least a hundred hens were hurled into a squawking uproar that filled the air with a snowstorm of white feathers. It wasn't difficult to see that this lot of chickens, brought to market, could easily go to meet their Maker more naked than clothed for the occasion.

Somehow I clambered aboard that truck and pried Frosty's fingers loose from a wire cage. Then, with him under one arm, I jumped back into the car and rolled up the window. As we drove away, I snapped, "If I don't get you out of here fast, little man, both of us are going to land in jail."

Frosty paid no attention whatever. I doubt that he even heard what I said. He was much too occupied with elaborately burping his Seven Up and playing with a handful of the biggest, whitest feathers he had ever seen.

A few days later, when I went to pay the grocer for that Seven Up, I parked a half block down the street—in front of a church.

5

WAY BACK IN June, when Frosty was still tiny, I had thought about the fellow and his coon I'd read about in a magazine. That man suspended from the ceiling, by strings, everything he ever expected to see or use again. What a good idea. Very practical. I didn't do it and *I should have*— right then. If I had, perhaps Frosty wouldn't have celebrated the Fourth of July the way he did.

The lemon verbena soap would never have slipped off the sink and onto the floor. Frosty would never have snatched it, and run off into the bedroom with it. As things turned out—with a hundred people waiting

for me to take them on a nature hike—I had to crawl
back under the bed to retrieve my coon because he still
had the soap in his mouth. And by the time I finally
cornered both the lemon verbena soap and Frosty, he
had worked up such a lather that he was beginning to
blow bubbles.

At first they were only small bubbles, but they got
bigger fast. When he ran into the living room to escape
both them and me, a whopper blew up in his face. It
scared him so badly he got hiccups. That caused his
bubbles to go both directions—outward in the traditional way, and backward, down his throat. The out-
board bubbles, in popping, splattered his face and
stung his eyes. Blindly he darted this way and that,
bumping into things and screeching for help.

Before I could go to meet my hike group at the
campfire bowl, I had to do a thorough hosing-out job
on Frosty. He fought me every step of the way, too.
Then I spooned some honey into his poor, irritated
mouth to soothe it, and dropped some olive oil in his
eyes to soothe them; his afternoon bottle soothed his
shattered nerves; and finally, completely exhausted he
fell asleep, which soothed me.

As I studied him, limp and peaceful on the pink
bedspread, I wondered how he could look that helpless
and innocent and so much like a little masked angel,
when he was such a perfect rogue. But that's a coon for
you. They know how. With them it's an art.

Anyway, the lemon verbena incident seemed to have
dampened Frosty's interest in soap as something to put
into his mouth to chew and suck on. Many times in the
weeks that followed he played with it, but only to make
that lovely lather to pat-a-cake in.

When I washed my hair, for instance, he always sat
on the wash basin, one leg around each side of a
faucet, and dabbled in the lather. Together we

scrubbed my head. While I took a bath, he occasionally ran off with the soap—just to tease more than anything. Usually he preferred to spend the time tight-rope walking on the rim of the tub or pulling on the chain until the stopper came out. I could never keep enough water in the tub to suit me. The last laugh was mine, though for he never failed to fall in at least once before I finished my bath. Such fun as we had! My cabin was in an uproar all the time.

Still, Frosty and I were working out a fine way of life together. He had completely turned his days and nights around to fit in with my various duties. Coons are nocturnal animals, but they also go abroad in the daylight hours whenever they feel like it. So Frosty's adjustment actually was no hardship for him. Moreover, he appeared to follow my schedule happily. In turn, I devoted every free minute to his upbringing and enjoyment—not only because I liked to, but also because I felt a real obligation toward him. You might say he was park property. He had been born within park boundaries; therefore, to a degree, he belonged to the public. As increasing numbers of campers learned about him, he began to have more public than he needed or than was good for him.

One afternoon, when the cabin was bulging with Boy Scouts, I thought of something which might simplify our lives.

Since the park was already full, that evening's campfire was going to be the largest of the season. Hundreds of people would be there. Then why not take this opportunity to introduce Frosty and all of his public to each other all at once? Maybe after that the two of us could have more time to ourselves. I walked over to Headquarters to talk it over with Roy Cushing, the Chief Ranger.

"Sure," he laughed. "Go ahead and try it. But I'm glad you're doing it, and not me."

I knew what he meant, all right. Most campers were fearful of any wild animal. If Frosty should fall in love with this audience, the way he usually did with people, and make a dash for some of them, we would have the granddaddy of all stampedes; and there wouldn't be nearly enough trees for everyone to climb.

"I know the idea's a trifle risky," I admitted. "But I'd sure like all our visitors to see what charmers some of our forest friends are. Talking about them is one thing, but actually having one there for them to see would be a lot better."

"That's for sure," Roy agreed, "but that coon of yours—"

"He's a lamb, Roy, really he is," I persisted. "And the people would enjoy Big Basin much more if they could only see who's around to visit them in the night. Those who have little fears would lose them, once Frosty turned on his charm."

"Or leave the park in the interests of self-preservation," Roy put in, cocking an eyebrow.

The coons already knew the campers, of course. Generation after generation of mother coons have told their young ones about these humans and the tasty snacks they serve in front of their tents after campfire. About the middle of August each year don't they bring their adolescent youngsters into the campgrounds, and teach them how to make the most of the golden summertime, when, because of the campers and their goodies, every night is party night?

After Labor Day the party season closes down, as it does in most parks over the country. Afterwards, whole families of coons wander about, searching through empty campsites for their people friends, and looking bewildered and forlorn. They just cannot understand why they are deserted so suddenly, when everything had been going so well. It always made me sad to watch them.

Mulling over all these things, I finally decided to give my nature talk on coons at this big Saturday night campfire, and have Frosty there at the microphone with me. Because a Park Naturalist doesn't often have a live specimen to hold as he speaks about an animal, its life and habits, I was more anxious than usual to give my talk that night. It was going to be a fine opportunity to show this huge crowd that there was nothing to fear from the furry ones who walked across their sleeping bags or drank the cartons of milk they left out on their picnic tables. They would learn that the dark hours of the night are a busy, enchanting time in this forest of giants.

They did. Thanks to a tiny coon named Frosty, the Big Basin raccoons were to live in style for years and years.

Before the campfire I took Frosty on my lap for a briefing and a heart-to-heart talk. Scratching him under the chin so he'd look up and pay close attention, I said, "Little one, listen to me. Listen carefully to every word I say." And I told him that there were vacationers camping in this redwood park of ours who neither understood, nor always loved, wild animals. I explained further that if we could help them know what interesting and friendly people coons were, then the young campers would no longer be afraid after their Coleman lanterns were out; neither would grown-up campers awaken and turn their flashlight beams this way and that every time a twig snapped. "We want them to rest, to enjoy all of their stay here, and to appreciate our coons," I reminded him. "Then they'll be good to coons everywhere."

Frosty seemed to be listening. His black, shiny eyes

searched my face intently as I spoke, although his soft hands never stopped feeling around over mine, fingering my ring, playing with the bottoms of my cuffs. I didn't actually know whether he understood everything I was saying or not, or whether he was even paying attention. You can't tell about a coon. They're much too smart to let you in on what they are thinking.

The campfire that night was a fine, booming thing. Some of the slabs of wood burning in it were as much as a husky ranger could carry. Tongues of flame leaped high and danced a ballet of vermilion design on the massive trunks of the redwoods. All the log seats were filled; people were standing as far as you could see, both at the back and along the sides of the bowl. Families laughed and chatted together; some of them on the outer rows huddled together under blankets, for Big Basin's summer evenings are chilly.

Waiting at the microphone, ready to begin, I couldn't help uttering a short but fervent prayer: "Dear God, please let them still be there when my talk is over."

At first I spoke of coons in general, then of Big Basin coons, who liked and trusted their human friends enough to visit their camps and hint for refreshments. Then I told them that within moments they would see one of our park coons, a little orphan we were raising. I asked them to be very quiet when he appeared, so he wouldn't get excited.

"He dearly loves people," I said, "but he's never been near so many, nor has he ever seen a fire." I felt like adding, "And if he suddenly dashes out to you and scrambles up one of your legs, just relax, and try to remember that all he wants is to feel the skin on your stomach." But I didn't. Instead, I nodded to Ranger Sholes, offstage, to release Frosty from his carrying cage.

Through the doorway my little coon saw me, and with a high-soprano trill of pleasure, rushed out. As one entity, the entire audience in the big, outdoor bowl half-rose off the log seats and gasped with delight.

I don't know just what they expected of a baby coon—what he would look like or what he would do—but it was easy to see that their hearts melted completely. Then remembering to help by remaining quiet, they settled slowly back onto the seats and watched breathlessly.

Had it not been for the popping and crackling of the fire, you surely could have heard a leaf fall. As I walked around on the rustic stage, Frosty bobbed along behind, a happy smile lighting his face. After a few minutes I picked him up, stepped to the mike, and went on with my talk—under difficulties.

"This is Frosty," I told them. "He's a raccoon baby—or kit—about two months old. He was orphaned here at Big Basin, and brought to me by a fine boy, who wanted him raised so that he could go wild when his time comes to seek a mate—which will be about the end of January, I imagine. When that day arrives, he will be free to do just that. Meanwhile, it's my job to see that he lives safely past the age when he is easy prey for such as coyotes and bobcats and horned owls."

While I was speaking, Frosty put on a good show. But he didn't know he was the star performer before one of the largest crowds ever to gather at Big Basin. He was too occupied with wrapping his arms around my neck and hugging me; he was too busy reaching inside my shirt front and feeling my skin; too intent on trying to undo the black tie I wore as part of my state park uniform. Out front, my audience was spellbound—but not, I'm sure, by what I was telling them.

I went on: "Coons are called the 'bear's little brother,' although they are only distantly related to the bear family. Actually they are more akin to the panda of Asia and the ringtailed cat of our own West. Certainly they have one of the widest distributions of any animal in America. They range from the creeks and ponds of the lowlands and foothills up into the lower edge of the pine forests, up to a mile or more elevation, down to the edge of the sea. You can find their baby-like hand and foot prints in the winter snows sometimes— and almost any time along the streamlets of the palm-lined canyons, leading from the desert at Palm Springs up into the San Jacinto Mountains back of the town."

By now I was having a time talking, and the audience was having a time concentrating on what I was trying to say. Frosty had climbed up onto one of my shoulders, and was sitting astride the back of my neck with a leg draped around each side of it. One of his hands gripped a fistful of my hair; the other ran an exploratory finger round and round in my ear. Just try to deliver a coherent informational talk with this going on. But I struggled with it. So far, Frosty was so occupied he hadn't noticed the campfire and the sea of faces out there. So I continued.

"Coons are one of the most omniverous of furbearers —they and possums and black bears. They eat almost anything, animal or vegetable. They like to fish in creeks, ponds, and marshes and search for frogs, small animals, birds and their eggs, crickets, and wild berries. But never carrion. That's no doubt one big reason why no coon remains have ever been found in the La Brea Tar Pits of Los Angeles. The coons weren't interested in the dead animals entrapped there, and they were much too smart to become entrapped, themselves. They—"

Suddenly Frosty saw the campfire. A log had popped

sharply, setting off a fountain of sparks that startled
and then attracted him. His exploration of my ear
stopped abruptly, so I knew he was staring, transfixed,
at the flames and, just beyond them, the hundreds of
faces looking out of the semi-darkness at him. The big
audience knew that he was aware of them now. After a
moment they began to talk among themselves quietly
but excitedly. Frosty had the undivided attention of
well over fifteen hundred people.

"Now," I thought, "This is the moment. Here is the
biggest audience Frosty will ever have. What will he
do? Sensitive as he is to the moods of his beloved
humans, will he go tearing out there to hug them?" I
had to be ready to move fast.

I might as well have saved myself all that worry.
Instead of going wild over the roaring fire and more
Public than most of us get in a whole lifetime, Frosty
was utterly overwhelmed. And who would ever have
expected such a thing as that?

All at once shyness engulfed him, and he ducked his
head down behind mine to hide. Reaching his arms
over my ears and around to my face, he gripped a
cheek in each hand, and pulled himself tight against
me. Then, holding on for dear life, he buried his face
in the hair on the back of my head. The world had got
too big for him.

As I talked on, I stroked his feet and legs and tried
to let him know that all was well, that there was
nothing to fear. Perhaps my voice speaking on calmly
helped, too. Anyway, I could feel him relax—enough
that pretty soon one of his hands shifted from my
cheek to my eyebrow, pulling it down so that it closed
one eye. At this the crowd almost forgot itself and
laughed aloud. A moment later they murmured a long,
admiring "Aw-w-w-w" in unison, when Frosty peeked
out at them very shyly. And as my nature talk on

coons progressed, he peeked at his public again and again, always ducking back quickly afterwards, as if he couldn't bear to look. Gone was the ham of all his past performances, gone all the swaggering cockiness. Frosty had fallen victim to abject stage fright.

Concluding my naturalist's talk, I said, "This big park, like nearly all vacation spots in our mountains and valleys where there are streams or ponds, is populated with coons. These coons are sociable. They like people and their things. They'll come to visit you if you invite them.

"How do you invite them? Go back to your camps and cabins after campfire, and light your lanterns, maybe even turn on your car lights for a while; get out your loaves of bread, your cookies and candy, your grapes and apricots and melons. Then take a spoon or something and beat on your frying pans and pie tins. The Big Basin coons will wonder what's up. And they'll be so curious they'll have to hurry to your lights to find out. All of a sudden you'll look up and see one—maybe three or four—out there at the edge of your circle of light, peering around one of the big trees or through the huckleberry bushes at you."

By this time all the campers in the log seats around the campfire were talking among themselves. I could see whole families conferring in low tones—planning what they would do later in the evening. By the orange glow of the flames their eyes shone with enthusiasm. I said to Frosty, "I think we're making friends, little man." He responded to my reassuring tone of voice by releasing my eyebrow and clutching my nose instead. Again there was a wave of half-suppressed amusement.

I finished my talk with: "Enjoy the coons tonight and every night. But let's all remember that Big Basin is their home, and that we are guests in that home."

So a good many campers saw their first coon that night. They saw him as something very real and understandable—and adorable. How could they ever have dreaded or feared him? The park literally burst with love and goodwill toward our forest friends. In the fifteen minutes we were up there on the stage, Frosty became Big Basin's Personality Boy—its Public Relations Department. I could see Roy Cushing and several of the other rangers standing at the back of the bowl, watching the crowd and grinning. Every once in a while they'd laugh and shake their heads in disbelief. This timid little fellow didn't seem to be the coon they knew.

When campfire ended, almost all the campers went back to their tents, lighted their lanterns, and banged spoons on kettles and frying pans to see if they actually could coax some of the coons into their campsite. The evening wasn't the quietest one on record in Big Basin, but none has ever been any happier or any more fun, for coons came from everywhere. They climbed up from streamside thickets; they climbed down from hollow oaks; they crawled out from under park houses and maintenance shops.

Just as I had predicted, they peered from behind the trees and huckleberry bushes and sniffed the air to find out if these city people smelled right. And if their noses didn't wrinkle up as if they were whiffing something long dead, a camper knew he had passed the test. He could now be sure he wasn't giving off any bad odor born of fear or hate. Once a camper received such a stamp of approval, he was on his way into coon society.

In almost no time, then, the coons would edge closer until they were within the circle of light. About this time their eyes would be gleaming expectantly out of the black masks they all wore. Each would be looking

like the Man Who Came to Dinner. Every one would be hoping his heart out that all these lovely people meant so well that he could wheedle them out of every last tasty morsel in their food lockers.

The park coons grew to be experts at this—magna cum laude. Year after year the campers handed over their best, and ate what was left. Into the soft, almost human hands of our beloved bandits went birthday cake, candles and all. Into those hands went the juicy red watermelon and the bunches of grapes from the Great Central Valley. As it turned out, the coons, not the campers, smacked their lips over the sacks of apricots and peaches, the cream puffs, and the Palm Springs dates.

And what did the campers do when they finally got around to eating? They just opened a can of Spam, and crunched on the stale rolls the coons had rejected. I tremble to think of how things could have been if some prankster had served our little friends some vitamin pills.

Open House didn't make the front pages of the newspapers, but it was a huge success. Afterwards, whole families of coons, warming to the new social whirl, deserted the park garbage cans in droves, and accepted invitations right and left. That night set the style for all nights to follow, for years to come—thanks to one tiny, scared Frosty.

6

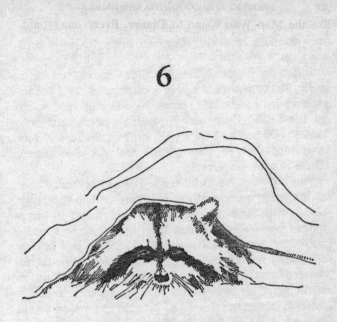

AS THE SUMMER season in Big Basin moved well into July, Frosty grew and filled out until he was as muscular as a small puppy. He had come a long way in the world, too, for now he had some famous people for friends. But the rangers he loved most of all. More and more of the men were stopping in to see him, now that he had wowed everyone at the campfire. Their visits became big events. Whenever he heard their heavy-booted step on the front porch, he would always hurry to greet them. Then in minutes they'd be on the floor in noisy roughhouse. To hear the coon growl and pretend to be fierce, one would think he meant to tear them to pieces with those sharp little teeth of his. But how they all enjoyed their mock fights.

Ranger Bill Weatherbee summed it all up one day:

"When this critter was small and on the bottle—that was woman's business. Now he's getting to be one of the boys."

I had to laugh. What Bill didn't know was that, while Frosty was now eating a number of solid foods, such as fruit and table scraps, he was still very much on the bottle. Every day he had his bottle, and was burped. Of course I didn't tell on him because it was important that he stay eligible for the select Inner Circle of park rangers.

Not knowing the awful truth, Bill and several others of the crew occasionally stopped by and took Frosty home with them to give him a real workout—man style. Upon being returned from one of these expeditions, the coon usually had just enough pep left to climb into my lap and snuggle cozily with his bottle, in the crook of my arm. Then, after a few swallows of warm milk, his eyes would grow heavy and gradually close; completely relaxed, he became as limp as a rag. In the last moments before slumber engulfed him, he'd whimper softly, all the while laboriously rubbing his ears, his head, and his chest until his arms were able to move no more. How he fought sleep! I think he hated to give up, and perhaps miss something.

When at last I laid him on the bed, and covered him with his blanket, no little coon ever looked less like a wrestling partner for a six-foot ranger. He was still a baby. He still needed his "mama" and his bottle, and lots of love and care when he was tired and sleepy.

Yet you couldn't have made some of my old-timer camper friends believe any such drivel as this. These were the trusting folk who asked why I didn't bring Frosty down to their camps the afternoons I had to work straight through. "It'll keep him out in the air and sunshine," they argued, "and think of the fun we would all have. We won't hurt him. Really."

They volunteered for the baby-sitting; I didn't sug-
gest it—or even encourage it. They kept right on
volunteering, too, although many times they must have
wondered why; for Frosty, in a swift sniff and a glance
or two, quickly got their number. He could tell they
weren't invincible like those big ranger fellows, who
were as used to wild animals as they were to their park
of giant trees. These campers could be bluffed. If you
merrily bit your initials all over their anatomy, you
could get your way about practically anything.

And that's exactly what he did. He cut his teeth on
some of the oldest, most experienced campers in Big
Basin. But when I'd call for him at the end of one of
those afternoon outings, he'd never give me an inkling
of this.

Recognizing the sound of my car, he'd always come
bouncing to meet me, grinning from ear to ear, and as
fresh as a young fern growing in the spray of a waterfall. The way he squeaked with gladness and gently
patted my face was heartwarming. He wore innocence
as naturally as a fawn wears its spots. The minute he
turned on that charm—presto! There before the eyes
was a furry cherub, and the brightness of his halo was
dazzling. That is, to me it was. But not to the coon-
sitters.

One of them, an elderly Big Basin old-timer, shook
her head and laughed as she watched Frosty pat my
face. "I can't believe it," she said.

"Believe what?"

"How he can look as if he'd been making mud pies
all afternoon."

"Hasn't he?"

"He sure hasn't. He hasn't even touched his pan of
mud. To see him now, you'd think he'd been sitting on
a pillow, meditating. My darling little granddaughter

doesn't have such an angelic expression on her face on Christmas Eve."

"What did he do?"

"Well, for one thing, he got in my fresh berry pie, and ate the middle out of it. Not one of the edges. He had to take the middle. That was just *one* thing." The family, grouped around her, nodded vigorously.

I plainly saw that none of them could understand how he'd got away with so much. Why, when I had brought him down to this camp earlier in the day, he hadn't even waited until I was out of sight before taking command. From then on, he did only what he wanted to do, and everyone attempting to change his mind paid for it. Several had tried, but they learned fast. For one thing, they couldn't keep a grip on him. Coons can turn halfway around in their hides, and every time Frosty did, his sharp teeth always left a mark in human flesh. Best to let him do as he wished and remain whole, everyone decided. It beat me, the way my camper friends, having discovered all this, continued to plead, nevertheless, for the privilege of being outwitted and bitten. They surely must have known they couldn't win.

There stood some of them now, in front of their tent—the chewed and the dazed, painted with mercurochrome and plastered with bandaids.

"What else happened?" I asked, as if I had no idea.

"He wanted to play with the silverware. We haven't located all of it yet."

"He took a notion to my bobby pins and curlers."

"He squashed all the tomatoes we bought yesterday."

"My flashlight—I tried to get it back before he wore out all the batteries."

But Frosty had had a pleasant afternoon out in the

fresh air and sunshine, gaily getting into things and biting people—and making them like it. Well, he did it with such joyous abandon. He made a festive occasion of it. With a mischievous twinkle in those shining black eyes, he mangled some of his most devoted fans. Yet these same people would make a date for the very next time I'd have to work through the afternoon. And afterwards they would again proudly show their scars. You have to have *It* to get that kind of date, and have a waiting list besides.

By the middle of August Frosty had grown into quite a coon. He was beginning to get his new coat of fur, and thanks to the more rugged rangers and a few friends with hides of leather, he was well-muscled for his size. The day finally came when he threw his bottle on the floor so hard it broke. That was the end of that. We put some of his baby things away for good.

About the same time, wild coon mothers began taking their broods out into the night for training. I could hear them after everyone had gone to bed and the park was quiet. Every now and then that long, high, quavering trill—so much like the Who-o-o-o-o-o of an owl—would slip into the silence of the redwood forest. It was querulous and soft—the coon's evening call. To me it was companionable—one of the night sounds I've always loved most.

I think park people are just naturally tuned in to the sounds of the wild. We are awakened from deep sleep by animal footfalls in the duff; we even detect their calls over the top of human hubbub.

Such was the case one August evening when some of us were enjoying the dance floor out in the forest, the other side of Opal Creek. Suddenly I saw Don Meadows cock his head for a moment, then hurry to the far railing and peer over the side. Signaling for Ranger Arlan Sholes to turn off the music, he called, "Come over here, everyone, but come quietly. I want to show you something." Arlan and I joined the hundred or so campers who went to see what Don had discovered.

There's nothing a Park Naturalist loves more than for Nature to put on a good show for the visitors. Don was no exception. He was really beaming now. And by the time we had all clustered around him, he was looking like the proverbial cat that swallowed the canary. Grinning broadly, he half-whispered, "I bet you've never seen this before. Look." He nodded toward the base of a huge redwood, only a dozen yards away.

We did look, and as one, gasped with pleasure, for there, illuminated by the lights of the dance floor, was a mother coon and five little kits. "She has them out on what is probably one of their first training tours," Don said.

The young ones were wobbly and unsure of themselves, but anyone could see they were eager about this expedition because their shoe-button eyes were bright in their black masks. They were so playful that their mother was hard put to get them rounded up and gathered around her for instructions. Completely fascinated, we watched.

"She's telling them what their evening lesson is going to be," Don explained.

Practical Arlan leaned toward me and asked in a low voice, "What's Don up to—mental telepathy?"

"Nope," I answered. "You know as well as I that he understands coon talk."

"How do you know what the mother is saying?" a girl asked Don suspiciously.

"Wait and see," Don laughed, neatly fielding her question. Then he caught my eye and winked. How often had we talked on coons at the campfire, always speaking of these August nights when raccoon mothers first bring their babies out for training. And how many times had a family of coons made an appearance and put on an exhibition for us? Exactly none. This night, I thought, will be one to remember.

"Hear Mama giving her instructions?" Don asked the group.

Everyone nodded, for her chirring and trilling were quite audible now. A moment later all the kits turned away from the family circle like football players leaving a huddle, and began to climb the big redwood slowly and laboriously. They had their orders, and there was no question in their minds just what those orders were.

Inch by inch the kits worked their way up the thick red bark of the old giant, while down below, Mama coached and called encouragement. They were awkward and shaky, of course, but they persevered; they managed to clamber up four or five feet—well above the flaring roots—before Mama decided that was far enough, and told them to back down. Four of the five obeyed at once, although timidly. At this, the mother glanced up at us who were watching, as if to ask, "Could yours do as well?" Our presence hadn't bothered her at all. She was going right ahead with her evening's chores as calmly and methodically as if they were out in the wilderness somewhere, far from human habitation.

Then we noticed that the runt of the litter was not backing down to the ground as the others were doing.

"That little guy—he's scared," a teenager exclaimed.

"Yeah, he's looking down. He should never do that."

The four kits, who were now completing their assignment, waddled over to their mother. The little one continued to cling desperately to the tree. We could

hear his trills of fear growing louder as he kept looking
down at the rest of his family safe on the ground
below. All of us groaned with sympathy. And we began
to worry.

"What's he going to do, Mr. Meadows?"

"Do you think he'll fall?"

"If he does, he'll get hurt, won't he?"

"It's only a few feet."

"Sure, but to him it's a mile."

Don betrayed his anxiety by shoving his Stetson onto
the back of his head, but he answered quietly, "The
mother coon will solve her problem. I imagine she's
had this one before."

Mama Coon did solve her problem, although not by
talking her least one down the tree. She tried to once or
twice. She called to him loudly and insistently—
probably assuring him that there was nothing to be
afraid of, and just to back down a bit at a time, as the
others had done. But he was too frozen with fear to
move. Besides, his arms and legs were getting tired; we
could see them quivering with the effort of hanging
on.

For Mama Coon the moment of decision finally
came. She knew she had to do something. Forthwith,
she left the rest of her brood and went up that tree in a
hurry. Her nails really dug into the bark as she climbed
to a place just below her frightened youngster. Here
she worked herself around so that she was crosswise of
the tree, her flank barely touching two little hind feet.
Don's face began to relax into a merry smile. "It's
things like this," he said, "that place coon intelligence
near the top in the animal world. Watch now."

We did. And I'm sure all of us will remember how
Mama coaxed her baby into putting first one and then
the other of his hind feet on her side so he could stand
on her and rest; how she moved downward an inch or

so, and lured him down just that much, so that once again he was standing securely on her flank; how, in this way—a little at a time—she lowered him safely to the ground.

Her brood once more assembled, Mama Coon evidently went over the lesson point by point, because they all clustered around her for a few minutes while she had her say. She even boxed some ears for talking in the huddle. Someone wasn't paying attention. Afterwards she led her family off into the dark of the forest.

Everyone who watched this small drama unfold learned a lesson in nature study far more heartwarming and permanent than any either Don or I could ever have presented at campfire. "Those coons are sure the high spot of my vacation," one man said.

"This is the first time I ever heard a coon talk," a girl said. "Wish I knew how to speak Coon Latin."

"Made me think of the briefing sessions we'd have before a mission," an Air Force veteran remarked, lighting his pipe. "*And* the de-briefing," another veteran added.

Don was ecstatic over the evening's turn of events. "Boy!" he exclaimed, "What we need around here are more coons to put on a show for us."

But such things rarely seem to happen when you most want them to.

One of the best demonstrations I ever saw of raccoon intelligence and the way a coon mother demands obedience from her young took place at my back door late one evening. Only Frosty and I witnessed it, but since the time had come for Frosty to be given an example of conduct by his own kind, I was glad that he, at least, was there. I think he gained something. Certainly he was impressed.

The old coon who lived under the house brought her

four youngsters up on the back porch for me to see. I had known they were under there, for I'd heard them moving around during the dark hours, sometimes banging their heads on the water pipes. Now, as they all sat peering in through my kitchen door, she talked to them constantly in that conversational way coons have with each other—and with those of us they know well. Then one of them said or did something he shouldn't have, I guess. Anyway, she lit into him, thrashed him there in public, and set him to crying. She had a few things to say at point-blank range, too, before herding her family off the back porch.

At the corner of the house she again reviewed the situation with Junior. For one thing, you bet, she warned him about what happened to little coons who didn't mind promptly and without argument. Coon mothers never stand for any nonsense. Either their young ones mind *at once*—or else.

Still muttering angrily to herself, Mama now led her family out into the darkness toward the creek to hunt frogs and crayfish—that is, all except Junior. He was benched for the evening. He was told, not asked, to remain there at home—alone.

How do I know? Well, that's where and how he stayed for the next two hours. And those were two *long* hours that he padded round and round my cabin, crying bitterly at the top of his lungs. He was broken-hearted. Yet made no move to follow the others to their midnight picnic. His mother had cut off his privileges, and it probably never occurred to him to disobey her. He had no interest in a second thrashing. He knew who was boss in the family.

Those hours were as awful to me as they were to Junior. I wanted so much to go out and comfort him and invite him in for something that would make up for the frogs and crayfish he was missing. But I didn't.

Having seen a good many human children who didn't mind, and were therefore obnoxious to other people, I appreciated what his mother was trying to do, and kept out of it. I just left the porch light on and my door open, and went out now and then to call encouragement to him.

Frosty listening in silence—and awe—to all the distress outside our house, seemed to grow up a little. Or that's what I thought that night. Next day it became abundantly clear that he had merely graduated to bigger things. He discovered some bathroom plumbing that had so far escaped his attention.

For the first time he appeared to notice the rush and roar of the flushing. Scrambling up onto the seat he looked down and watched the swirling waters bubbling and churning. Wow! This was even better than Opal Creek; and right there in the house, too. Until then he had been too small to climb so high. Frosty was growing up.

What a happy smile spread over his masked face as I pulled the lever and flushed the toilet once more to show him how it worked. This time Frosty reached down into the whirlpool and splashed gleefully. I saw it dawn on him that here he had a creek of his own—a private Babbling Brook. "Well," I laughed, "it's true all right. The best things in life are free."

But they weren't—not quite.

About a week later, on a Saturday while I had a group out on the Maddock's Cabin Trail, there was a kind of crisis in Big Basin. A wrought-up picnicker ran all the way to Park Headquarters to report it. "Say," he blurted to the Chief Ranger, "do you know that the faucets in the Picnic Area are almost dry?"

"They can't be," Roy Cushing answered. "Just last night we checked the tank on the hillside—the one that supplies the Lodge, the Picnic Area, and several ranger cabins. It was okay then."

"Well, sir," the man insisted, "it must be empty now, for there's hardly any water coming out of the faucets."

California had been having serious drought troubles, and Big Basin was often low on water. Sometimes we wondered if one or more of our five sources of supply were going to fail completely. But not this one, surely. Not with water coming into the hillside tank the night before. Nevertheless, Roy and another of the crew went down to the Picnic Area with the man to take a look at the faucets.

What the man had said was true, all right. Only a trickle was coming out of them, and already several hundred picnickers were there wanting water. Hundreds more would arrive before noon. Saturday was always a big day in the park. Breathing a prayer, the two men hurried back to Headquarters to organize a work party. Because there had to be water in that tank, there must be a leak or stoppage somewhere in the water lines. They must lose no time in locating the trouble, wherever it was.

Quickly the two rangers took off up the hill to check the tank. The water was low again, to be sure, but there was a moderate flow coming in through the intake from the spring. Apparently the source was producing, although not fully. So for the next hour they went over the pipeline, following it down the slope, then into and all over the Picnic Area.

But the mystery of the dry faucets only deepened, for not one leak or stoppage could they find. The trickle from the faucets wasn't nearly enough to supply the wants of the 2500 or so people who would be using the picnic sites before the day was over. The two rangers were beginning to work up a sweat as time passed, and they could see cars by the dozen rolling into Big Basin. This was all we needed for another wild Saturday—a park full of people, and only a dribble of water.

Inspecting the water pipes leading downslope out of the Picnic Area, the rangers gradually approached my cabin. Still they had discovered no cause for water failure, and they became more and more mystified and worried. Near my back porch they sat down on a log to cool off and think what to do next. It was then they heard it—my toilet flushing one time after another.

"That's funny," one of them said. "Harriett's out on the trail, and isn't due in for another half hour at least." The toilet flushed again and again—then again.

"What do you make of that?" asked the other ranger.

"I can't figure."

"This I have to find out about because I *know* she's not home. I saw her start down the Maddock's Trail with a big group an hour ago."

That did it. Both men ran to my back door and let themselves in with a pass key. Dashing to the bathroom, they got there just in time to see Frosty stand on the toilet seat, pull the lever—and jump in.

He had discovered the Father of All Waters. He had learned how to make his own riffles to play in any time he liked. Such Heaven! Such joy! As the water swirled and gurgled around him, his masked face, neatly framed in the white oval, beamed up at them happily. It's a good thing Frosty was as big as he was before he discovered this noisy little pond, or he might have disappeared through his own genius.

Moving with dizzying speed, Chief Ranger Cushing put an "Off Limits" sign on my bathroom door— printed in coon language. To me he boomed, "You keep that brat out of your bathroom. He's come close to draining the park of about a fifth of its water supply. We can't afford a drought and an educated coon at the same time."

Assistant Ranger Clyde Newlin thundered, "If I ever catch Frosty around any of our waterworks again, I'll countersink him in the forest floor."

I could see what he meant all right. After that, I not only closed the bathroom door, I locked it, knowing Frosty and his high Coon I.Q.

7

FALL CAME AT last. No longer did the park teem with vacationers. The campgrounds were almost empty now, except for a few retired people who didn't have to get children off to school or report back to a job. The crew, finished with the long hours of summer, put on fatigues and began their Winter Work Program. A couple of us—I, for one—remained in uniform at Headquarters to do office work and talk with the several hundred sightseers who would come daily—as long as the weather was good—to stare open-mouthed at the redwood giants. On weekends there were always picnickers from the Monterey and San Francisco Bay areas, but for the most part, Big Basin by day was quiet and tranquil; by night, as silent as a remote wilderness.

The forty or more deer, finding almost no one to pester in the camp areas, now wandered forlornly around Park Center. Their fountain of groceries gone, they once again eyed the garbage cans—but with no enthusiasm whatever. Already licking the discarded paper plates, crunching apple cores and pieces of mouldy buns, were the raccoons. They, too, had no other choice. Gradually then, most of the animals went back to their own natural foods until another summer rolled around.

As dry September gave way to the falling temperatures of October, the forest gradually changed. Along the creek banks, the big leaf maples, the hazel bushes, the willows, the alders, and the rosettes of azalea all turned yellow, touching the scene with sunny patches of brilliance and gaiety. On the steep hillsides of the canyons, poison oak daubed the monotonous green with splashes of flaming foliage. At the upper borders of the redwoods, whole woodlands of madrones glowed. On open slopes and ridges, toyon berries began making their appearance, and then turned from scarlet to deep crimson. Here and there, the broad domes of the California buckeye, their boughs white and bare since late August, were clusters of pear-shaped pods that were breaking open and freeing their seeds. In September, an old friend, Ethel Young, happily accepted an invitation to come join Frosty and me at the park for as long as I would remain that fall.

When she arrived she was met and overwhelmed by the furry head of the house, who immediately registered his approval by ramming a hand down inside her blouse as far as it would go. For a minute I held my breath. You never really know your friends until something like this happens.

I needn't have been concerned. It was love at first sight for both of them, so that day we embarked upon what was to become a thoroughly enjoyable association.

Once in the park, Ethel was invited to help out a few hours a day in the gift shop. I continued with my chores, only now that the pressures and responsibilities and long hours of summer were over, I had more free time. No more campfires to organize and direct of an evening. No more guided nature hikes to lead occasionally on weekends. Mostly what I did was see that the live exhibits in the museum were fresh and labeled, take care of some of Roy's paperwork, spend time at the Information and Registration window at Headquarters, and perform other small duties as needed.

Frosty kept the house—upside down.

Down in Park Center, we couldn't help noticing the bark on our few madrones. Thin as paper, it kept peeling off in featherweight curls. Naked now, the cinnamon-colored trunks and limbs, so bright in contrast to the somber backdrop of evergreens, appeared to be twisting and straining upward toward the sun more than ever. Their curves gave graceful relief to the huge, dark boles of the Douglas firs and the grey-lavender columns of the giant redwoods, so skyscraper-straight and tall. And wherever the madrone's clusters of red and orange berries swung from beneath their broad, highly-polished leaves, there was a gleam of warmth in the shadows—rather like a ray of light passing briefly through a stained glass window, giving life to the darkened interior of a cathedral. In summer, the evergreens unquestionably dominate the forest; in the fall, the deciduous trees have their moment of glory. Autumn is a good time in redwood country—or almost anywhere, for that matter.

We loved it. Together, Ethel and I tried to help Frosty enjoy it, too. During the day, at least one and frequently both of us took him for a romp, either through the deserted campgrounds or down one of the little-used park roads. Sometimes we went for a hike on one of the park trails that bordered a stream. When we did, we never hampered Frosty with harness or leash. Such a thing would have been utterly senseless. We couldn't have got rid of him if we'd tried.

Many an afternoon after work we pretended to be on vacation. Only a stone's throw from our back porch was the Picnic Area. By midafternoon almost any autumn weekday, we had it to ourselves. How we loved roasting weenies and toasting marshmallows in the stone fireplaces, and eating off the huge redwood plank picnic tables—just like the park visitors we had envied all summer. We thought it especially nice after sunlight no longer brightened even the loftiest treetops, and dusk had begun to lower. In the gathering night, the coals of our fire always seemed more companionable than at any other time.

Yet we weren't alone. One is never really alone in the forest. Drooling expectantly over our shoulders was always a deer or two—perhaps a doe with twin fawns or maybe a couple of our big, antlered bucks. On the table corners perched the stellar jays, squawking as usual, eternally waiting for a chance to snatch something—a potato chip or a hot dog, with everything on it. Sitting on the bench beside one of us, Frosty watched our uninvited guests with only casual interest. He was much more intent on the edible part of our picnic, and he never failed to eat his share.

The share of a healthy, five-month-old coon can be considerable. All his hikes, swims, and wrestling bouts

had made him strong and hefty for his age, and constantly hungry, besides. We couldn't fill him up. With all this, and the spoiling he got, too, his happy good nature expanded to include everything and everyone he saw. He was agog about the world and everything in it.

By the end of October the days had grown crisp and cool, the nights really cold. All sounds had become sharp and clear—the loud crack of the woolly tanbark oak acorns that landed on our steeply-pitched roof, rattled all the way down, and plunked onto the ground; the taunting squawks of the jays as they quarreled with each other, and pestered the chipmunks, desperately trying to hide their winter supplies; the chipmunk's screeches of rage.

Now autumn winds were filling the air with clouds of tiny seeds, loosed from millions upon millions of redwood cones slightly larger than a marble. Flat sprays of foliage were drifting down from the treetops far above. And in Big Basin the treetops are far, far above—for many of the mighty giants of this climax forest are higher than a city block is long! Often their upper trunks disappear in the fogbanks that roll in from the ocean; sometimes their tips are lost in the low, fluid clouds of winter.

About Thanksgiving, the rains usually come in great drenching downpours. Early that December, a gale howled down from Big Basin's rim, swooping in among the mammoth trees, shaking and swaying them to and fro as if they were grasses on a vast prairie. In their torment they creaked and they groaned, and their limbs began plummeting to the forest floor—limbs as big as some of the pines people camp under in the Sierra Nevada. Redwoods in summer are awe-inspiring to view. Redwoods in the rainy season, when the ground is soaked and the winds high, are fearful, indeed, to live under.

In winters past, ranger houses down in Park Center had been partially crushed by mere limbs; some had been completely flattened by falling trees. All the crew except the Whittakers and ourselves had moved up to Flea Protrero—a meadow where it was safe.

About nine o'clock one evening, it seemed better to leave Big Basin than to stay any longer.

8

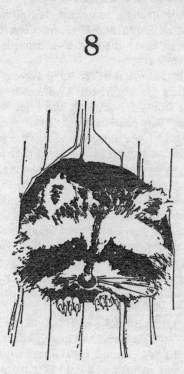

WE KNEW THE storm was coming. The Weather Bureau had predicted it. But we had no idea exactly when it would get here, or that it was going to be so severe.

Early the morning of the day it struck, Roy Cushing knocked at our door. "I think we're in for it," he said, indicating the sky.

"Today?"

"That's what the Weatherman said. Heard it over the radio while we were having breakfast."

"Did he say about when today?"

"Well, near evening sometime. It's already pouring up at Jedediah Smith and Crescent City. Craft warnings are up all along the central and north coast. You girls better clear out."

"Is it going to be that bad?" Ethel asked.

"I wouldn't be surprised. You never know what these winter fronts are going to turn into. Best to be on the safe side," Roy cautioned.

So Ethel and I got to work and packed many of our things, which we stowed in the car. From time to time we stopped to pat Frosty, who was playing with half a dozen blue jay feathers I had picked up the afternoon before and brought home to him. A moment of decision was facing us, and we knew it.

After working for a couple of hours, we stopped to have a cup of coffee and warm ourselves at the potbelly stove. While standing there, sipping our hot drink, we watched our half-grown raccoon entertaining himself—unaware that we were all fast reaching a crossroads.

"Come on," I said dully to Ethel, "Let's take Frosty for a walk. Let's go down to Opal Creek." I think she guessed what I had in mind, for she said nothing.

The day was so grey and cold that we put on extra sweaters and jackets before starting out. But the crisp chill of the air filled Frosty with more than his usual pep. Leaping and bounding along beside us, he chased leaves and redwood foliage that the wind had set swirling through the forest. Sometimes he vanished into a redwood crater, and peeked out at us from behind one of the huge, rolling roots. Other times he galloped on ahead, glancing mischievously back over his shoulder as if to make sure we noticed all his capers. He was having great fun. We weren't. Our thoughts just then were far from pleasant.

"Do you have any idea he'll do it?" Ethel asked, eying the leaden sky and trying to be casual.

"No," I replied, "but he has to be given his chance. Once again he's in Someone Else's hands."

Opal Creek didn't look inviting that day, even to Frosty. He ambled slowly out onto some boulders, pushed aside the big woodwardia ferns and horsetails, and dabbled a finger or two in the water. But he didn't reach under the rocks for crayfish or minnows. Instead, he investigated a hole under the exposed and sprawling roots of a streamside wax myrtle.

"Now," I whispered to Ethel, "Now, while he's busy."

Fists clenched in our pockets, hot tears stinging our eyes, we turned back toward Park Center. Quickly we moved out of sight behind a fallen giant and, completely hidden by its massive bulk, walked resolutely and grimly away.

It didn't work. Thank goodness it didn't work! On two wheels Frosty rounded the upturned root system on the far end of the big tree, and met us head on. I think he knew full well what we were trying to do. With that stricken expression in his eyes that I have seen many times in the eyes of wounded animals, Frosty looked from one to the other of us—and began to cry softly and pitifully, for he was uncertain now that his family loved him any more. Working his hands together as any of us might if we were in great agony of spirit, he seemed to be pleading, "You *wouldn't* go away and leave me! Don't you love me any more?"

Did we! Of *course* we did. When the heart melts, so also do firm and good resolutions. Ethel and I sat down in the duff, as damp as it was, and had such a joyous reunion with Frosty that anyone witnessing it would surely have thought we had been separated for weeks and weeks.

"I guess you aren't ready to go yet," I told him, "but when you are, just say so, and you'll be free."

Then, with the little fellow looking back every few steps to make sure we were still there, the three of us headed for the cabin and the warmth of our wood-stove. What would come next we didn't know. Perhaps the storm would veer away from our mountains. Even if it didn't, perhaps it still wouldn't be too bad; perhaps we could safely stay down among those giant trees for a while longer. I felt—as I always do—that we would be guided in the course we should take. One thing we did know: whatever was to be done, all three of us were going to be doing it.

When we reached the house we found a note under the front door. My friend, Mina Kelly, had telephoned the park and left a message: "How would you folks like to come down to Southern California and look after our ranch while we go to South America for a few months? Let us know."

The Kelly Ranch, a big one of a hundred acres in oranges, lemons, walnuts, and avocados was located about four miles out of Santa Paula, near a river. As Ethel glanced at me, I couldn't help smiling. I was remembering that the wide wooded riverbottom provided homes for many animals, including coons without number. I was also recalling the deep ravine that connected the ranch with this well-watered wood-land. The more I thought about all this, the more I had to smile. We looked at Frosty. He seemed to be smiling, too. But then, wasn't he always?

I went outdoors and studied the sky. Since our return from the hike, the already heavy clouds had dark-ened so much that the two old spike-tops over toward the campfire bowl stood out white and ghostly. Night was threatening to close in at just half past three. I could see the redwoods were swaying back and forth in such long arcs that I wondered what kept the towering, incredibly slender shafts from falling across one another like so many jackstraws. Somewhere over in the direction of the South Campground I heard the splintering crash of an enormous limb as it tore loose from some giant, fell perhaps 300 feet, and slammed onto the ground. There would be more of these tree-sized "widow-makers" before long.

At this point it became painfully evident to me why the ranger crew always moved up out of Park Center to higher, warmer, safer homes in the upper meadows and more open forest when winter came.

"What do you think?" I asked Ethel, who had walked out on the porch and was standing beside me. "Shall we sleep on this, and decide tomorrow whether to leave or to stay?"

"Whatever you say," was her somewhat dubious reply, for she knew that all the ranger residences down in Big Basin, except ours and the Whittakers, had already been closed. Besides, I was free to leave the park at any time. By now there was little for me to do. Only on weekends and nice weekdays, between downpours, did many tourists come in to see the redwoods. Because of Frosty I had hesitated—and still was hesitating—to leave Big Basin for the year. I so wanted him to go wild there.

We went on packing, nevertheless, and we didn't sleep on it, for the storm worsened rapidly.

About seven o'clock the gale descended on us in full force. Every few minutes we could hear the wind gather itself together up there on the rim, and then come roaring down the mountainside with the thunderous scream of a jet. Shortly after eight the sky opened up. All of a sudden our roof sounded as if a thousand buffalo were stampeding over it.

A new moment of decision was at hand. Within a

few minutes our problem had become one of making up our minds whether to remain in the cabin, among the falling limbs and trees, or to gamble on a dash for safety through three miles of massive redwoods, up and out of the Basin, to a meadow. There we could be out of reach of the tallest trees. I didn't have to say all this to Ethel. She could see how things were. She knew as well as I that in our indecision, we had waited just a little too long.

"How do you feel about it now?" I asked her finally, knowing the answer.

Before she could reply we heard it start—that dread sound of the redwood forest—that ripping *cr-r-a-a-a-ck!* which can knife through the shriek of a winter gale as sharply as a rifle shot can pierce the stillness of a desert sunrise. It literally paralyzed us where we stood. It paralyzed Frosty, too. The stuffed sock he had been playing with dropped from his hands as he froze. Instinct, and perhaps even memories of early summer, were telling him what this was. And it could be that he felt our terror—our helplessness at not knowing where the tree was, which direction it was going to fall, or how far it would reach.

"Stand still," I said to Ethel. "No use running out." And there wasn't.

For long, shattering moments that seemed to stretch on and on into forever, the giant went through its final struggle to live. All the terrible storms of yesteryear it had endured; this one it would not survive. The shallow roots, losing their grip in the rain-softened earth, were slowly letting go at last. But after nearly twenty centuries of holding fast, they would not give up easily.

Again and again the tall timber split. Higher and higher up the massive bole the crack widened as new gusts of wind whipped the crown of green back and forth through the sopping clouds. I could feel my blood turn to ice when the deciding blow of the battle wrenched the old giant free of its earthly home, and started it on that long journey to its last resting place. Out of ages past came a deep, sorrowful moan, as down, *down,* and *DOWN* it crashed, dying with the terrible roar of an approaching express train; carrying firs, oaks, and laurels to their doom as it fell. We could hear these lesser trees snapping like so many twigs, being crushed into woody bits.

Then came the mighty shudder of the ground as the redwood struck. The cabin shook as if some monstrous, unseen hand had yanked it off its foundations. The floor jarred so violently that the three of us were flipped up off it. The roof jolted in such a way that the smokestack from our potbelly stove came loose, rolled all the way down the steep pitch, and broke noisily over a small stump beside the house.

I think it was a full minute before Ethel and I could get our breath back. The first thing she did then was to gather Frosty up in her arms and comfort him. And he comforted quite easily. To be pressed against a warm body, and to feel strong arms around him, holding him tightly, was assurance that this world was still intact.

I said, "Now?"

"Now," Ethel replied resolutely. "And the sooner the better."

"Then get yourself and Frosty into the car," I ordered, my voice sounding unnatural and tight. "I'll dash over to Whittakers and find out what they're going to do."

I took off through the trees.

In moments I was back. The answer had been simple and final. "We're staying," Mary had told me, shrugging. "As long as Mel can look out the window and see the Oakland Tree still standing, I guess we'll be right here. He's gone to bed."

The Oakland Tree, one of the mightiest in the park stood within a stone's throw of their bedroom window. The Whittakers had already gone through other winter storms such as this one. So also had the big Oakland Tree.

Quickly taking on the gamble of escaping from Park Center, we locked the cabin, although I can't imagine why, and jumping in the car, sped past Headquarters. On up the narrow, winding road, through the deserted park we went, cautiously and fearfully. What we had to do now was to dodge falling stuff on the avenue of the giants, along which we were hurrying. I concentrated on holding the car in the middle of the road as we plowed through the driving rain. Ethel held Frosty, and with her window open, peered into the gloom up and ahead in hopes she could spot any falling limbs— or trees—in time.

Without a doubt, this ride was the most harrowing of our entire lives. Our chances of getting out of Big Basin intact were something less than 50-50, Ethel and I knew that. All we could do was keep moving, and hope that we could make it up the Summit Meadow. Frosty, sensing our danger, snuggled against Ethel, tucked his head inside her jacket, and clung tightly to her shirt front. Only once in that wild dash to safety was anything said out loud.

"Hold up!" Ethel ordered tensely.

I hit the brake. A crooked limb, almost three feet through, had just crashed onto the pavement dead ahead, and was splintering all over the road. Following it earthward was a rain of redwood and Douglas Fir foliage that clattered onto the car, and bounced off. Again we all but stopped breathing.

But we survived that close one and several others.

We twisted and turned like a warship on a zigzag battle course as we tried to avoid the windfalls that littered the highway. All the while we were praying that none of those still dropping from above would hit us.

None did. Dented, but unhurt, we climbed up that spiraling road to the patch of open country, where even the tips of redwoods a block away couldn't reach us. Hundreds of times I had crossed here on my way down to or back from Santa Cruz. Often I had driven up to Summit Meadow just to find out how warm the sunshine was, or to see what the sky had in mind. Down in Big Basin, at the bottom of the tall, dense redwood forest, one could never tell about such things. Now, of course, we weren't wondering what the sky held for us. There would be no silvery moon or glittering diamonds up there to set off the silhouettes of the forest that night. All we were interested in right then was the luxury of open space with nothing more than grasses, coyote brush, and manzanita standing in it—and nothing whatever leaning over it.

Despite the inky blackness, Summit Meadow had never seemed so wonderful. We were grateful for the comfort it gave us throughout the long, stormy night. Our hearts were so full of gratitude that, for a long time, we couldn't speak of it. Instead, we turned our attention to Frosty who, after I had pulled up, came climbing across my lap. He wanted to look out of my rain-pelted window to see where we were, and what was going on. But there was nothing to see but water pounding on glass, and when I turned out the lights, there wasn't even that—just total darkness.

"How about going to bed, little man?" I asked, cuddling him and scratching gently behind his ears. That was fine with him. Whenever he made up his mind to anything, he always went ahead with it without further ado. So now he began his bedtime ritual of rubbing his face, his ears, the top of his head, and across his chest. I knew when he gave up at last, for he became dead weight in my arms. In the darkness I had to smile.

"Tonight could have been so different," I whispered, remembering the events of this afternoon that seemed so long ago. Yes, it could have been very different. We might have been alone up here—without Frosty—and he alone down there, in this terrible storm, among the falling trees.

Throughout the endless, black night I held him. Huddled together for warmth, Ethel and I tried vainly to sleep sitting up. Every few minutes the wind would die down to a low, whistling moan—just enough to lull us into drowsiness. Then, driven by power from the sea, it would come howling up the canyon, snatch the car, and shake it with the vicious ferocity of a bobcat killing its prey. Steadily, without letup, the rain drove horizontally against us, first from one direction and then the other.

As daylight streaked the leaden sky, the downpour stopped at last—for a few hours, anyway. We didn't wait to see how long.

"Well," I said to Ethel, "looks like we've been given the word to go south with the birds—today."

She gave me a long look. Another decision stared us in the face. In the middle of it sat Frosty, beaming and plainly inquiring, "When do we eat?"

Ethel fell to considering her situation as I leaned back and tried to assess my own. We were both teachers, and we both expected to resume our profession the following fall. Before then, I planned to complete assorted freelance writing and art work. Ethel hoped to do some substituting until summer, when if she chose, she could return to the Big Basin gift shop as I rejoined the park crew in late May.

Meanwhile, why not the Kelly Ranch? For me it was a part of a familiar scene among friends and family and close to the rural school where I had taught so happily for a number of years. Frosty could go wild from there as easily as from Big Basin. The sycamores and oaks of the nearby riverbottom wouldn't be as spectacular as the world famous redwoods he had always known, but for a little coon they offered much more. Branching at all angles, they seemed to beckon wild ones into their protective hollows. All at once I felt at peace with the whole idea. Quite simply and clearly, a door had opened as another had closed.

I interrupted Ethel's thoughts. "I think you'd like Southern California," I ventured. "And I'm sure Frosty would like Ventura County oranges. Shall we call the Kellys? We can finish up at the cabin and clear the park in an hour or so."

"Fine with me," Ethel replied with enthusiasm.

Frosty was sitting on my lap contentedly pat-a-caking and studying first one and then the other of us with eyes that sparkled. He always appeared to know when new adventures were being planned for him.

9

THE 350-MILE trip downstate from Big Basin to Santa Paula went smoothly. At Santa Cruz we had breakfast and telephoned the Kellys. We told them we'd accept their invitation—providing it could include one adolescent raccoon, who might change the ranch all around to suit himself. Not knowing everything we did, they laughed and agreed at once. "Of course you may bring the coon," John Kelly said. "The house is big, as you know. There's plenty of room; he can't hurt anything. We'll be so relieved to know that the ranch is in good hands. Then we'll be free to enjoy our trip."

I glanced at Frosty, whose hands were busy exploring the coin return slot. Then and there I made up my mind that his hands were going to be good—or else.

(Or else what?) We'd make certain they wouldn't wear out our welcome at the Kelly Ranch.

"We'll come then," I said.

"Can you come today? We'd like to take a plane from International this afternoon."

"We're on our way now, John," I laughed.

The town clock said eight on the dot when we got into the blue Plymouth and headed south.

Later in the morning we stopped for gasoline at a station on the edge of Atascadero. Immediately we let Frosty out to play on the grassy lawn back of the station. The proprietor took one look at him bouncing like a rubber ball, yelled, "Hey! Wait a minute!" and then ran for his house. In moments he emerged— carrying a coon the same size as Frosty.

The way the two ran headlong toward each other reminded me of those jousting tournaments of King Arthur and his noble knights I'd read about as a youngster. In the middle of the lawn the coons met with such a thud that both were hurled back, panting. But for them it turned out to be a big day, because neither had ever played with another of his kind before.

Bursting with delight over each other, they wrestled and romped around the green for the next hour. I don't know who had the best time—they who played so joyously, or the three of us who watched. When it was all over, both coons stretched out limp and exhausted in the cool grass. Neither seemed to mind when he was finally picked up and carried from the scene. Frosty slept the rest of the trip to the ranch.

He awakened as we turned down the long dirt lane between the walnut and citrus groves late that afternoon. Ethel helped him sit up and look out the window. "And so begins chapter two of your life," she told him. But he appeared not to hear her, for he was busy watching a new kind of tree go by—a bushy tree with orange-colored balls hanging all over it.

Never one to be bashful about beginning new things, Frosty jumped right out of the car after we stopped beside the big, two-story house. "Casing the joint" with one sweeping glance, he took instant note of a huge avocado tree nearby. In no time he was up the trunk and out on one of the sprawling limbs.

Now this was a tree one could climb and enjoy! Those at Big Basin were not to be shinnied up lightly. From his perch in the fork of the big branch, Frosty surveyed the rows and rows of trees on every side, as if to say, "I didn't know you could look *down* on a tree."

Laughing at his bewilderment, we went out to the garage to get the key to the house.

This ranch was a second home to me. I had been in and out of it for years, for the Kellys were dear friends of long standing. I knew that their two grown sons, who had a ranch up the road a few miles, would be doing the farming. Our main job was to act as ranchhouse, dog, and cat-sitters.

How good it felt to be in a real home instead of a leaky mountain cabin; how good to be warm and dry—and, above all, to be out from under those giant trees! Nothing is more icy and sopping than a redwood forest in winter; nothing pleasanter and milder than Southern California during these same months.

"Well—time to move our things in," Ethel said. "Time to start making a farmer coon out of a park coon."

He "made" very fast. In fact, at that very moment the transformation was under way, for Tuffy, the Kellys' Scottie dog, had heard us arrive. Trotting briskly toward the house to see who the intruders might be, he had already plunged into a cadenza of hysterical barking. Now he came bobbing noisily along under the big avocado tree intent on fulfilling his obligations as Guardian of the Property. Not for one second did he suspect unidentified objects overhead.

Suddenly something green, smooth, and roundish plumped onto his back. It thumped an already high-C bark into a falsetto shriek, and sent him scooting in pain and surprise. *What* was this? With eyes bulging, he retreated under a pyracantha bush to recover his wind and wits. Then, bouncing around like a rubber ball, he charged out into the open to raise all possible cain in defense of his home.

Tuffy could explode into such an uproar that any man or beast would find blessed relief in getting away where he didn't have to hear it. By the time Ethel and I got out the back door, the Scottie had discovered his attacker up in the avocado tree; and he was making it brutally plain that no blankety-blank coons were wanted around there.

Then it happened again. Playfully, and with only the friendliest of greetings intended, Frosty selected and picked another avocado, threw it at his host—and connected a second time. Tuffy's outrage now boiled into a full head of steam. Meanwhile, Blackie, the big old Persian cat, had taken one look around the corner of the house and was fleeing to quieter, safer places. Our ranch life was off to a flying start.

It was a good thing Tuffy knew me well, or he might have had a stroke that afternoon. Because he did recognize me as an old friend, he finally let us soothe his hurt feelings and entice him into the kitchen for a bowl of dogfood and a hambone we had brought him. Gradually his blood pressure returned to normal. No doubt the thought occurred to him that this animal must be someone we knew, or we would have run him off the place ourselves. Still he grumbled under his breath, as he lay down on the hearth in front of the crackling fire I had built, to digest his dinner and gnaw on the bone.

"Come on," Ethel whispered, making for the back door, "Let's bring Frosty in."

We had a time, of course, coaxing him out of the low-branched lookout he had appropriated for his own. But finally he clambered down and allowed himself to be carried into this house that was so much larger than any he had ever seen before.

"How do you suppose he'll like Tuffy?" Ethel queried.

"All I know is that he doesn't eat cats," I answered. "Or didn't, anyway. He's never met a dog before."

"Do you think they'll fight?"

"I imagine we're about to find out. We'd sure better move with care. Keep the hose handy."

"In the house?"

"Well, not quite," I retorted, "but let's sneak Frosty in while Tuffy's busy; and for heaven's sake, tackle that little problem tomorrow, when we're all rested and full of breakfast."

"And in good humor."

So we did. We spirited Frosty into the kitchen and fed him. Then we let him walk round and round on an inspection tour, feeling the stove and refrigerator, the cupboard door handles, and the legs of the kitchen stepladder. We held him up so he could see the faucets run. Together we watched the swinging pendulum on the wall clock, and talked about it. Then, two closed doors separating us from the Master of the House, we wrapped Frosty in his blanket and took him and his ring of keys into the back bedroom which had been assigned to us. Gently we laid him on the huge four-poster bed and sat down beside him.

But Frosty wasn't ready to sleep just yet. He was

finding the newness of his surroundings pleasantly disturbing—the huge bed, the light fixtures, the dresser with its mirror, the windows with their frilly, white organdy curtains. I finally had to go to bed with him so he could settle down for the night.

For a few minutes he sat there wide awake, looking all around, idly playing with his string of keys. I could see that he was wondering. Never before had he been in such a house; never before had he failed to hear and smell his deer friends, walking around in the dark, outside. He wasn't sure what it all meant. But with a big dinner inside of him, he did not care quite as much. With us cuddling and loving him, he was feeling more secure and contented all the time. Gradually the unfamiliar things ceased to be as strange and before long nothing seemed more important than his own comfort. He decided to lie down on his back and rub his head and chest for a while—anything to stay awake.

Finally Frosty could fight sleep no longer. Heaving a contented sigh, he turned over and snuggled up to my back. "Tomorrow is another day," I thought. "In the light and warmth of the sun things will look different— to both coons and Scottie dogs."

10

SURE ENOUGH, ALTHOUGH rain still pelted Northern
California, the sun was shining in Southern California.
Things did look different.

In a happy mood, Tuffy bounded into the kitchen
for his breakfast and slurped it down as if he had only
the usual things on his mind. Then he set out on his
daily route through the orange and lemon groves with
the air of a gentleman farmer who has important projects under way, and intends to supervise them closely.
Jogging pertly down an irrigation furrow, he sniffed at

certain trees where he might expect to pick up canine messages. You would have thought nothing more than a few stray ladybugs had ever crossed his path. Blackie had her breakfast, too, after which she retired to the chaise longue on the patio to clean up.

Frosty also appeared to be at peace with the world. Stretched out full-length in the big bed, his head on one of the pillows, he slept soundly until nine o'clock. When he finally ambled into the breakfast room, he looked like any young man in the morning, before he has combed his hair and had his coffee.

Later, when he was fully awake and fed, curiosity set in. After exploring all the rooms on the lower floor of the ranchhouse, he sat for a long time in the living room, which spread across the front of the house, gazing through the picture window at the lawn and flower garden. Never before had he seen the likes of red poinsettias in full bloom or the bushy trees in neat rows just beyond; he had never known the brightness and warmth of so much sunshine. He was utterly enchanted. For an hour or so he basked there in the morning sun and looked at the array of pretty things growing outside.

He was even more fascinated with the upper floor of the house. Discovery of the stairway opened a new world to him. From the top of the stairs he could look down at us—something really novel and exciting. So he turned that spot into a handy lookout station. In the time it took us to climb the steps, he could hide in any of a dozen secret places. Sure, we tried closing the doors to the bedrooms, hall closets, and bathroom; but none of the latches worked, and there were no keys. That second floor was made to order for an inquisitive and mischievous raccoon. I lost track of the number of trips we made up and down those stairs between breakfast and lunch that first morning.

"This coon's going to wear me out," Ethel complained. "If I were in training for the Olympics, it would be different."

"He has to get acquainted with his new home," I argued. "And pretty soon he'll have to get acquainted with Tuffy and Blackie."

"Not so fast! Let's take care of the simple things first."

A few minutes later we heard a muffled crash overhead.

"Now how did he get up there again?" Ethel wailed. "I just got through shutting him in the back bedroom."

"A coon is never really shut in anywhere as long as the door has knobs to turn," I reminded her as we hurried up the stairs, two steps at a time.

In one of the hall closets we found Frosty, beneath a stack of hatboxes and a heap of animated coats and jackets, screeching at the top of his lungs and threshing around in terror. After we dug him out, he streaked past us to the stairs and rolled all the way to the bottom. For several hours he was content to leave the upper floor strictly alone.

"What are we going to do with you?" I shouted through the back screendoor at him, for he had hurled himself out of this den of booby traps.

"You'll have to admit the Kelly Ranch is quite a change from the drippy redwood forest," Ethel pointed out. "And sunshine livens you up; makes you feel like doing things instead of huddling around a potbelly stove. Here you can even see all the sky you want without going outdoors and dislocating your neck. Besides, this isn't exactly a mountain cabin we're in. It's enough to overwhelm a little coon, or anyone; even me. Give Frosty a few days. He'll settle down and figure out how to act in a big, ten-room house on an orange ranch in sun country."

He did, only he didn't take that long to do it.

Back indoors after lunch, Frosty once again gave the interior of the house a quick once-over. To make himself feel more at home, he did splash in the upstairs toilet for a few minutes before streaming water all the way downstairs and through the kitchen to the back door.

Now that he had checked out all the indoor facilities, he was ready for a look at the runty forest, standing in rows all around the house. Pushing open the screen, he galloped into the avocado orchard and disappeared from view. He was gone for some time.

Meanwhile, Tuffy, with that "mission accomplished" look, came trotting home from his inspection tour and stretched out on the back lawn to rest. But he was not at ease. Something was prompting him to sit bolt upright. His wriggling nose swung his head this way and that, searching the airways. Suddenly he stiffened. A moment later, Frosty came leaping and bouncing happily into the yard after a bee he had been chasing. At the end of one of his long leaps was Tuffy. Nose to nose they met.

It was a shock, all right, even to the dog, who had seen the whole thing coming. And poor Frosty! All in one wild second he landed, saw his predicament, and executed a backward roll to safety. Then, bristling with alarm and breathing heavily, he flattened himself and went into a shuffling retreat, the way coons do when they get ready to defend themselves. At this, Tuffy launched a series of ear-splitting barks.

Ethel and I had been washing out a few clothes in the service porch tubs, so we were right there and saw it all. Fortunately, we didn't rush out and try to interfere. "We've got to keep out of this if we can," I whispered. "Let them work it out. But if worst comes to worst, there's the hose over there by the cellar door."

As we watched this meeting of two traditional enemies, beads of perspiration broke out on our faces. What if these two beloved pets suddenly flew at each other and became locked in a death struggle? We had a bad moment there.

We needn't have. The Scottie backed slowly into the shelter of an elderberry bush and, eyes skinned back, stood trembling. Frosty, hump-rumped, head and ears leveled against his shoulders, growled deep in his throat. But with the passing of a little time, doubt set in: with Tuffy, doubt that the masked foreigner over there had any real desire to rip him to pieces; with Frosty, doubt that the dog's bite was as bad as his bark—How could it be, anyway?

Our coon's warning growls soon began to lose their fire. In almost no time they turned into muttered remarks that served mainly to bolster his own morale. Moreover, he relaxed so much that, although he continued to study his black, shaggy adversary over there, he let his restless hands explore the grass all around him, and even crumple some dried-up sycamore leaves. They fingered, they probed, they sorted. Every now and then they came up with a bug or two to chew on. Yet not once did Frosty take his eyes off that apparition under the elderberry bush.

Hour after hour the cold war went on. Ethel and I took turns leaving our forward observation post so that gradually, albeit under difficulties, the household chores could get done.

On and on we waited; on and on the Scottie and the raccoon waited. The rest of the day they waited—sizing each other up, taking each other's measure, trying to appear nonchalant and unconcerned. Tensions were easing, true, but one careless move by either of them, and no telling what would happen.

As the winter afternoon waned and supper smells came wafting out of the kitchen, coon and doggie stomachs began to be more bothered than their suspicions. By then no kind of a scrap would have interested Frosty anyway, for doubtless the thought had occurred to him somewhere along the line that here was a new audience to play to. And hadn't all audiences loved him? Of course they had. Well then, there was nothing to be disturbed about, after all. We watched fear and uncertainty die in him; we saw love gradually replace it and fill his heart to overflowing.

This warming trend, however, received small encouragement from across the lawn. By the hour Tuffy sat in haughty silence. Evidently the Scottie was one landholder who just wasn't used to having newly-arrived, smart-aleck guests bombard him with his own avocados. And while he had long ago ceased to bark on the subject (why waste your energy on such rabble?), he obviously intended to snub his visitor. With spine ramrod-straight, he gazed into the distance.

So it went for two days: Frosty busting out all over to be friends, Tuffy coldly aloof and unbending; each giving the other a wide berth whenever they met—one reluctantly, the other as if he expected to make a career of it.

As the third morning got under way, Frosty's feelings appeared to be hurt beyond repair. Never before had he failed to melt even the most hard-hearted. Never before had anyone shunned him and made him feel unwanted and unsure of himself. On the contrary, his winning ways had always triumphed; all comers had eventually told him how darling he was. They had hugged and patted him and scratched behind his ears. His shining black eyes, searching their faces, had never seen anything there but smiles and approval and admiration—all for him. His own heart, responding, had swelled with pleasure and desire to love them back. Now, for the first time he was meeting the monster of Rejection, and it was like a bleak wind out of the Arctic. To be so cruelly ignored crushed his gay spirit. It left him lonely and miserable. He didn't know what to do about it.

Finally, out of desperation I suppose, he began circling the Scottie. Somehow he must find a way to soften this granite. Tuffy, not inclined to be softened easily, neither moved nor let on that he noticed. By midday Frosty's circles had grown so small that they necessitated his moving with the greatest of care, lest he trigger something catastrophic. For Ethel and me, all of this maneuvering was fast becoming just plain hairraising.

In our anxiety that day we forgot about lunch and remained at the window, where we could see what finally would happen.

"Something's going to pop," I predicted, "and soon."

"With my blessing," Ethel added. "Almost anything is better than this."

We had very little longer to wait. On one of Frosty's next rounds he accidentally brushed the tip of the dog's tail. In that electric moment, Tuffy stiffened and growled in protest. Frosty hurtled backward, end over end, as if he had just touched a high-voltage wire. But a moment later, not to be denied, he was back at his circling again. Another round trip, and then another, slowly and hesitantly. He was trilling now—experimentally, hopefully. Who could mistake that lilt in his voice? Or resist it?

Then, quite unexpectedly, he stopped within pointblank range of the dog's face. Still nervous and uncertain, he was nevertheless ready to risk life and limb to win this glacial critter with the overhanging eyebrows. This was a supercharged moment that hung precariously between peace and war.

Completely baffled and crushed, Frosty began to trill again, plaintively this time. Then, with the warmth of one who had always loved everyone he met, he reached out with both hands and gently patted both of Tuffy's cheeks at the same time. Pat, pat, pat—nice and easy, with the tenderness of one who unmistakably offers friendship.

Now who could be so stony-hearted that he wouldn't respond to the baby-softness of a coon's hands? Who could resist such humility, or fail to forgive little lapses like the throwing of avocados? Well, Tuffy couldn't— although no one ever tried harder. In spite of himself, a shiver of pleasure rippled through his whole body and set his tail to wagging. And the faster Frosty patted, the faster the dog's tail wagged. Before long it was sending bits of grass flying in all directions.

That did it. All at once Tuffy's resistence crumbled before so much devastating charm. With short, happy yips, he erupted into a noisy but undying devotion that was to last as long as he lived.

As the tensions of the past two days suddenly let go, a feeling of tremendous relief flowed over both Ethel and me.

"Thank goodness that's settled," I said, turning toward the kitchen and some lunch.

"Yes, thank goodness," Ethel agreed limply. "But will you please tell me why man can't manage as well as a little coon does?"

"I wouldn't know. What do you mean?"

"Why can't he pat a few cheeks and melt a few hearts? Forget his deadly game of quick-draw. Why is that?"

"You've got me there. As far as I'm concerned, he can start any time. We can use more brotherly love."

"This kind?" Ethel laughed, beckoning to me to come back and look out the window. I got there in time to see our coon ride the dog through the geranium beds and down the driveway.

All afternoon the Day of the Big Thaw, the two mauled each other. By the hour they rolled, they wrestled, they chased, they ambushed and they tackled. Happily they grunted and growled and showed the whites of their eyes. Once they grabbed Frosty's stuffed sock and pulled in opposite directions until it tore apart. Then they chewed on it together until only shreds were left. After that they chewed on each other.

Around and around the house they tore, then around and around the barn, then out into the orange grove and back a dozen times or more. When all this grew old, into the house they romped, along all the hallways, through all the rooms. Clinging to each other they even tumbled downstairs. The entire house became their racetrack. Finally, as Ethel and I were preparing supper, they dropped exhausted on the front room rug. There they lay in two panting heaps—weary beyond any thought of food.

Pleased over this turn of events, I brought in several eucalyptus logs and built a fire in the fireplace. As soon as the flames were crackling warmly, Ethel and I sat down to a leisurely meal and a look at the evening papers. We became so absorbed in the day's news that a long time passed before we were aware of the silence. All at once Ethel noticed that there wasn't a sound of any kind anywhere. "Something's wrong," she said, putting aside her *Chronicle*. "It's too quiet around here."

"You are so right. Where are they?"

"I don't know. I don't hear them."

"What you suppose they're up to now?"

"Come on, let's find out."

We didn't have far to go, for we found them the first place we looked. We opened the door leading into the living room, and there they were, both of them. On the hooked rug before the blazing fire, lay our two little innocents, sprawled out asleep, snoring softly. Tuffy had stretched as far as his stubby muscles would let him. Frosty was lying with his head on the dog's flank. Neither of them heard us; neither moved; both were completely out.

"Can you beat it?" I whispered. "Who would have expected this?"

We eased the door shut, and went back to our newspapers. Later, after washing dishes, we too went in to enjoy the fire. Still Frosty and Tuffy slept on, waking only occasionally—just long enough to heave big, long, contented sighs.

Such utter tranquility we were to enjoy many an evening before the fireplace in that big living room— but only after wild, wild days. Of these there were to be many.

11

THE NEXT FEW days were like that one had been—filled with rough, noisy romping all over the ranch and through every room in the house, the hallways, and even the basement. To watch it was fun, but sometimes we were hard put to keep out of the way.

"Guess these two were made for each other," Ethel laughed, hugging the kitchen wall so that the puffing, blowing mass of fur could scamper by.

Once a thumping commotion sent us rushing to the stairway in time to see Frosty and Tuffy tumble from the top to the bottom. Until they bounced off the last step, they never lost their grip on each other. But neither was hurt. Yipping blissfully, Tuffy scrambled to his feet and raced down the hallway; Frosty caught up with him, leaped aboard, and as a double-decker they slid the rest of the way into the den—on Tuffy's belly.

Tuffy was more energy than brains. Frosty had plenty of both. After the matching of muscle and brawn got old to him, he contrived various kinds of tricks whereby he could match wits. Few wild things can beat a coon at this; certainly nothing domesticated can. Even a human has all he can do to compete successfully. So Tuffy didn't stand a chance. He was too trusting and much too feather-brained for his own good. Yet he was so pathetically eager to please his jolly playmate that he continually fell victim to Frosty's well-laid plots.

More than once he found himself looking down into a deep hole he'd been digging, and wondering why he'd dug it. Somehow, with the passing of time, the reason had become obscured. Perhaps it was because he wasn't able to remember that only an hour or so previously Frosty had led him to this spot and, eyes glowing, had then scratched furtively in the loose soil. Tuffy, watching, had thought he detected something secretive in his pal's manner. The longer he watched, the more suspicious he became that the coon was about to unearth a choice bone.

Never one to let others beat him to a bone, Tuffy had bolted at Frosty and shoved him aside. With the breathless excitement of the true prospector, he had begun to mine. Frosty waited only until the ground-breaking ceremonies were over and the excavation well under way. Then, unnoticed, he trundled off through the grove toward the house. By leaving Tuffy to pant and yip and grunt for an hour, he could have some uninterrupted time to himself.

He found many things to do. Now that he was

growing up the possibilities were practically endless. A huge ranchhouse was his to explore from basement to attic; assorted farm equipment was his to examine all he liked; a hundred acres of fruit trees were his to scale. We watched Frosty take to farm life and subtropical flora with even more enthusiasm than he had shown for park life and the redwood forest.

Well, after all, this was understandable. These bushy trees with their low-branching trunks were easy to climb. Frosty couldn't get enough of them or of the irrigation furrows, when they were running with water. I suppose they reminded him of Opal Creek. Only instead of there being just one big stream, here were lots of little ones. Narrow ribbons they were, side by side in rows, making liquid music as they trickled the length of the grove. None were more than a few inches deep, and Frosty couldn't find any fish in them, but heavenly days! they ran everywhere. Down in each were all kinds of stones to turn over and over, for citrus soil is loose and rocky. Many times, when Ethel and I went out to pick a few oranges and lemons for the house, we found our coon busily playing in the water, having fun trying to hold back the flow with his hands. He puddled in those furrows by the hour. Sometimes he even rearranged them.

I remember one day when he did.

I had been gleaning under a bare-limbed English walnut tree for unharvested nuts to put in a cake. All of a sudden I had the feeling that I wasn't alone. I glanced up to see Raul Martinez, one of the ranch hands, leaning on his hoe. Doffing his hat, he smiled with a wide expanse of beautiful teeth, and spoke softly. "Mes Weaver, I think your coon, she got no savvy about the irrigate."

"How's that?" I queried, knowing instantly that Frosty had done something he shouldn't have—again.

"Well, she puts me dirt in this places when it gots to go in that places."

I was at loss to understand, as Raul soon saw. Still smiling broadly, he went on with friendly patience, showing me with his hoe, building a small ridge of dirt, neatly, just so. "The water, she is rolling along fine. Bueno."

Thoroughly puzzled, I nodded, and waited.

"Then here comes the coons. She is good company. I like her. We make big laugh together. But then, when I turn the back, she make like this"—swarthy hands in the dirt now, bending the ridge in a different direction. Looking up, Raul flashed another smile at me and shrugged his shoulders.

"Frosty turned the water flow?" I asked—as if I needed to.

"Downs, downs, downs—into the barranca," Raul answered, demonstrating with his hands. "Our head of water, she go overboard from the last row over there. Verdad?"

I knew the barranca. It was one of those natural gullies that meander downslope from rolling hills to riverbottom. Ventura County, much of which is gentle uplands and stream-cut valleys, is seamed with them. Almost all ranches, whether they be cattle range, citrus groves, or flat beanlands, have at least one or two. During the wet season they many times carry run-off enough to make howling torrents of usually bone-dry riverbeds. During the long Southern California dry season, they are homes and runways for all kinds of wildlife—quail, coyotes, foxes, even an occasional mountain lion or bear.

Here in December our first hard winter rains were yet to come. The countryside was much too dry, and no two ways about it, the Kelly Ranch needed every drop of that precious water a citrus rancher receives when his turn comes to irrigate.

"I fix now," Raul went on. "But the coon, she fix him back. So, plop! Down into the barranca she goes again. Es muy mal."

It sure was *muy mal*. Water supply in Southern California at any time is precarious. Here Nature seems to be in revolt against man for building cities on poorly watered semi-deserts, and spreading vast, incredibly ugly subdivisions across fertile lowlands she had marked for growing food. All we needed—and that's about all we did need in Ventura County, to upset the balance of nature that year—was one coon from the well-watered big-tree forests to waste our already scanty water resources. Frosty, it appeared, had a weakness for playing fast and loose with such things. "I'll take care of him," I promised.

Like Old Dutch Cleanser I strode across that orange grove, with Raul right behind me. Stepping carefully over one running furrow after another, we soon reached the scene. There, just as Raul had said, a handcrafted ridge was funneling a stream of irrigation water down into the thirsty brush of the barranca. As you might guess, no coon was in sight. But there was no lack of telltale hand and foot prints. The freshest ones indicated a retreat across the grove, one row down. You can bet that from some hideout under an orange tree's skirts, Frosty had peeked out at us as we headed purposefully toward his latest engineering feat. The scamp!

I left Raul to restore the damaged channel and, following the prints in the dirt, I strode back across the grove. On the way I paused here and there long enough to repair places where little coon hands had either diverted or dammed the waterflow. Opal Creek had been one thing, this was quite another. This was California's agriculture Frosty was tampering with. The shenanigans had to stop. Now.

I trailed him to our back steps. There he sat, basking in the sun, looking as guiltless of any wrongdoing as a choirboy singing the *Ave Maria* in the Sunday morning service. Nevertheless, for the next five minutes, in simple but pungent English, I explained what we definitely did *not* do on the Kelly Ranch. For emphasis, I repeatedly jabbed a finger toward the grove and the barranca. I knew my eyes flashed fire, that my voice had a cutting edge. I also knew that he understood exactly what I was saying, and that I might as well go bake my cake.

There was one thing about Frosty: for all his maddening mischievousness, he was patient with me. No matter how upset I got with him, no matter how loud I boomed, no matter how exasperated or furious I became, he never failed to forgive me afterwards, and let me do all kinds of things for him—to make up for my momentary lapse of good humor.

This day also, he waited for my anger to spend itself. He permitted me to shout every ultimatum I could think of, and get all the old steam out of my system completely. Then after I had sat down on the step to calm myself, he crawled into my lap. With the sweetness of a child who wants more than anything in the world to blot out all unlovely sights and sounds, he wrapped his arms around my neck and clung to me. And while my stony heart was melting, he let me guess whether he was asking for forgiveness, or whether he was forgiving me. That's the way our heart-to-heart talks always ended—and the way Frosty went right on doing as he pleased.

I would like to meet the genius who, in matching wits with a coon, has ever won.

That winter Raul earned his pay. But for the first time he had a trainee-assistant—me. It was the least I could do. Fortunately Frosty didn't rearrange the irrigation furrows every time he decided to take a vacation from Tuffy. He found many other things to do. For example, he loved to slip into the basement of the house and wait for an unsuspecting mouse to come along. Then he'd snatch and play with it. Most people would have declared that his hunting and meat eating instincts were coming out at last—but that wasn't so. He never intended to kill and eat any mouse. He didn't even intend to hurt one. He just liked to massage them and model them into different shapes. Their furry bodies were so soft and warm that he loved the feel of them—and so he finally felt them to death.

When they no longer moved, he'd sit beside them, looking sad. He didn't understand what had happened to this little thing, that it wouldn't wriggle and squirm for him anymore. Death was beyond his comprehension.

The day we heard the white leghorns squawking and thrashing around down in the chicken yard, Ethel and I moved fast. Remembering the incident at the Santa Cruz market, and knowing about a coon's taste for fowl, we set out on a dead run.

"This *would* have to happen!" I shouted, as I rounded the corner of the barn and made a beeline for the chicken coops. At that moment there was no question in my mind that our coon had at last grown up to catching his own dinners. I could just see the Kelly prize hens being carried away and eaten. And not by a predator from the riverbottom either, but by one that was hand-raised, and living in solid comfort in the Kelly family home. "Hurry!" I yelled, "We've got to save those hens."

By the time we reached the coop, the chickens were

wired for sound. Squawking with all their might, they fluttered this way and that, colliding with one another and the sides and roof of the pen. Feathers flew in every direction. It was a scene of pandemonium and uproar such as I hadn't witnessed since that day in my childhood when a circus elephant escaped and went barreling down Main Street. Yet every Kelly chicken, however terror-stricken, was not only alive but in the best of health.

Frosty? There in one corner of the pen he sat, flat on his bottom, one arm wrapped around a big, fat hen, who was hitting the high C's like a fire siren. All the coon was doing with his hen was pulling out a few of her tail-feathers to play with.

Ethel and I stopped in our tracks and stared, not quite believing what we saw. Coons are famous—or infamous—for their raids on chicken yards. That we knew. But here was one who either hadn't heard what his kind was famous for, or else just didn't hold with senseless killing.

"Thank goodness," I muttered, when I saw that all the hens were never safer. Then I thought, "What will he do after he goes wild? Have we, with our good farm food, taken away his natural instincts for hunting?" The idea was a jolting one.

Unaware of our presence, Frosty let the hen go even before we got the pen door open. Then he did what he'd always done with feathers—sat and tossed them in the air. On his face was such a happy smile. His intentions toward that chicken—in fact, all chickens— had been purely honorable all the time.

As it was in the case of the Kelly rabbits. We ran pell-mell to "Rabbit Row" the first time or two we heard the thunderous stomping of hind feet on the hutch floors. Knowing coon ways, we could see Frosty reaching up, grabbing a rabbit's foot, and dragging it down between the slats so he could chew it off. Wrong again! Eyes gleaming with joy, he was under the hutches, all right, but with his fingertips he was having a picnic, tickling the bottoms of those furry old feet until the rabbits were slowly going mad. As long as Frosty was with us, the rabbits never suffered from anything more than wildly tickling feet. But *how* they suffered.

Blackie had her troubles, too. She barely tolerated Frosty anyway, and made a point of keeping out of his way. When they did meet, she hissed and spat in his face if he carried his teasing too far. What angered her more than anything else were the times he sat in her bowl of milk.

A bowl of milk is not a good place to sit, although Frosty liked it; by sitting there he could infuriate the cat. He thought it great sport to see her back away, glaring out of those great harvest-moon eyes as if she were going to fly at him and rake his face with her claws—and to gamble on whether she actually would or not. To live this dangerously was high adventure. He loved it. So he'd sit there, looking smug.

Blackie was no fool. She knew her bowl of milk was under that furry hunk of smart-aleck coon. Not quite having the courage to tackle him, she'd look to us for help. Somehow we were never fast enough to move Frosty before he had impishly fouled the milk.

He even pestered her as she tried to nap in her chair in the den. She'd no more than get settled on the worn-out sweater left for her comfort than Frosty would head in her direction. Stealthily he'd creep under her chair. Because an arm of the sweater always seemed to be hanging down, how could he resist taking hold of it, and pulling? He couldn't. He never jerked it, you understand. Instead, little by little, he dragged it out from under the cat.

At first all of this mystified Blackie. Then she peered over the side and saw what was happening. After that she fired hefty jabs at Frosty's merry smile. Sometimes he saw one of these jabs coming and ducked; other times he wasn't quick enough, and her lightning-fast claws hooked the sensitive knob of his nose. We knew whenever it had happened. He would have hiccoughs. He always got them when suddenly and unexpectedly he was frightened or hurt.

We'd see him bounding toward us at a gallop, hiccing loudly, thoroughly miserable, as he tried his best to outrun this thing that whooped up out of his throat every few seconds.

"Get the paper bag," we'd say, and stop whatever we were doing long enough to get one and make him breathe into it until he was rid of his annoyance. For a time, then, he'd be quite ready to let the cat alone and go find someone else to tease or some new mystery to investigate.

A number of the mysteries Frosty tried to solve yanked him loose from his curiosity temporarily; what's more, they nearly separated him from a long life on earth. For example, he just couldn't rest until he found out what those two little holes in the dining room wall were for. He kept at them, too, in spite of spanked hands, until he finally succeeded in working a fingertip down into one.

Thank goodness Ethel was nearby when it happened.

From clear down in the furnace room I heard her shouting my name. I could tell by the urgency in her voice that something was very much amiss. Two steps at a time I came up out of the basement and dashed into the dining room. There I found my friend sitting cross-legged on the floor, holding Frosty in her arms and rocking back and forth. He was out cold.

"What happened?" I asked, kneeling down and beginning to massage his icy hands.

"The light socket—over there on the wall." Ethel groaned by way of explanation. My heart skipped a beat.

"He isn't dead!"

"I don't know. He stiffened out—then"—nodding down at his inert little body; Frosty was as limp as anyone would be who had just plugged himself in on 110 volts.

"He lit up like a neon sign," Ethel told me, as we worked frantically over our coon.

It was touch and go there for a few minutes. But at last Frosty gasped and began to move his hands around over his chest, the way he did when he was drowsy.

"Thank goodness," we both mumbled, so relieved we could say no more. In another moment Frosty's eyes fluttered open, and he looked up at us as if to ask, "Where am I?"

We told him where, and that he was safe and loved; we held him and fussed over him; we did everything we could to help him recover from his shock. Like a person drugged, he shook his head to clear the cobwebs and get his eyes focused once more. Gradually he regained full mobility. But for a long time he was content to be cuddled and reassured. When at last he fell asleep, exhausted from his terrifying experience, we laid him on the bed in the back bedroom and tiptoed out. Best to let him sleep off his latest escapade. Later on he would awaken sufficiently to figure out something new to brighten his day—and ours.

That afternoon, though, Frosty decided against an electrician's career. Thereafter he bypassed every electric outlet in the house as if he expected it to reach out and yank him down into one of those two little holes.

He reminded us of a small boy hurrying past a haunted house after dark.

It must be true that both small boys and coons have guardian angels. We never doubted that Frosty had one, and that his was dedicated to the continuing indestructibility of his little charge. This was proven the following Saturday, when we cleaned house.

No one enjoys the din of a vacuum cleaner. The Kelly vacuum frazzled Frosty as nothing else ever did. The first time he heard it, he forgot about the dresser drawer he was rearranging and came charging down the hallway all a-bristle. Taking one look at this wheezing, whining monster, he attacked it as if it were his mortal enemy and he sank his teeth into the cord. The vacuum, however, had no intention of being subdued so easily. It spit back at him, then bit him viciously, and rolled him end over end into the corner. From then on Frosty feared the critter, and never trusted it again.

Just once afterwards did he ever get close to it, and then purely by accident. That was the morning he sneaked into the hall broom closet to hide from Tuffy. While he was waiting among the mops and brooms for the dog to come along, so he could jump out and surprise him, he glanced over his shoulder. To his horror he saw the awful thing standing there behind him, towering over him, all ready to pounce. The way he burst out of that closet you'd have thought a fire-breathing dinosaur had nipped off his tail down to the third ring.

Now Frosty should have been afraid of the refrigerator, and wasn't. Not a bit. He not only didn't fear it, but he came to look upon it as his favorite ally. Beneath it was a refuge from the dog and cat, who wouldn't have followed him under there for the world.

They had better sense. And it was a refuge from us, too. We also had better sense.

The big refrigerator was a wartime model, made of inferior and makeshift parts, as were so many appliances during those years. Day after day it threatened to quit, so everyone coddled and babied it. Long before we came, it began to overheat. To correct that, John Kelly had crawled under it and removed the housing from around the motor. So there, in all its glory, was the fan, whirling away like a buzz saw, ready to slice into nice thin strips anyone daring to venture too close. Well, nothing went under there anyway—then. But, now it was different, for here was Frosty. Not one to hesitate just because this dark cave was inhabited by a metal beast that could make confetti out of coons, he not only went under the refrigerator, he even slid under on his belly when he was in a hurry.

The first time he disappeared under there Ethel and I aged ten years. It's possible he might have, too. But at that moment he couldn't afford to be choosy about a sanctuary. We were hot on his trail; any hiding place had to suffice. He knew we were intent on a conference about this dastardly business of opening cupboard doors and dabbling in the black shoe polish stored there. Apparently the fan, no matter how terrifying it must have been, was preferable to doing time in the den, in solitary, the rest of the afternoon.

Flat on my stomach on the linoleum, I reached slowly and gingerly under the refrigerator with the idea of pulling Frosty out before the fan should whittle his rear. But his high coon I.Q. was equal to this emergency, you bet. As my hand inched toward him, a sassy grin spread over his face, as slowly and gingerly he began to back toward the whirling blades. His was the warning: "One inch more and I'll throw myself into this meat grinder." Not that he would have. But my own I.Q.—not nearly so high as his—told me only that I was facing defeat. I had to admit that this was a round Frosty had won, and always would win, every time he tried it which, after that, was several times a day, whenever he found himself in a tight spot.

12

DECEMBER IN NORTHERN California, especially in the heavily forested central and north coastal mountains, is much different than in the southern part of the state. There, in the redwoods, as much as 125 inches of rain has been known to fall in a single year. But down here we lived in a year-round climate that is usually more deserty than anything else. Even in midwinter Southern California gets the Santa Ana—east winds that blow for days on end, and sometimes for weeks. They blot up practically all the moisture, leaving a humidity of five percent or even less. Most of the time, though, the days are pleasant. The sun shines warmly until late afternoon, when the cooling fog rolls in off the sea.

From December until April it rains from 5 to 20 inches or so. Periodically, a classic flood rips up the countryside and dumps the best topsoil into the ocean.

When cold does come to Southern California, and temperatures drop into the middle and upper twenties, crews of ranch workers, bundled up in mackinaws and woolly caps, get out in the night to fire the smudgepots and turn on the wind machines to keep the citrus from freezing. Even so, there is a winter every now and then so severe that the most heroic efforts do not save the fruit.

In the days of not so long ago, before freeways and subdivisions and shopping centers spread over the most fertile and productive hills and dales, the landscape was a patchwork of apricot, walnut, and citrus groves. Our long river valley, sloping gently toward the Pacific, was quiet and pastoral and beautiful. We loved every square mile of it. Life there was good.

In January, singing Mexican-Americans began picking the bountiful crop of big, golden navel oranges, which remained on the trees of some groves, sweetening in the sun, until as late as March. Each May and June they started bringing in the juicy valencias. Throughout the year, every four months or so, they harvested the lemons. Not until September, after the heat of a long summer had ripened and dropped the English walnuts, did entire families of migratory workers move into the grove to fill the gunnysacks.

Ethel, Frosty, and I arrived at the ranch more or less in between crops. Except for the gleanings one could salvage from the ground under the trees, the walnut crop had long ago been processed at the Diamond "nut house" at Saticoy. The navels and a crop of lemons

were slowly ripening, but the avocados, approaching
full size, were maturing, a few every day. They were a
great source of delight to all of us.

About a week before Christmas, a gale howled in off
the ocean and blew fifty or sixty avocados off the tree
in the back yard. When we went out to gather them the
next morning, we found toothmarks and small chewed
places in almost every one. Frosty, Tuffy, and Blackie,
and no telling who else, had helped themselves, sam-
pling each in much the same way that some people
pinch fruit in the market before selecting what they
want to buy.

There is something about the bland, fatty goodness
of avocados that attracts many animals. A rancher
nearer the hills than we had trouble with coyotes picking his crop. They did it intelligently and methodically,
neatly biting off the avocados easily reached and laying
them out in rows in the open so they would ripen
faster. They even partially covered them with dirt and
leaves to prevent sunburning—and perhaps discovery
by the ranch workers. At night the animals would come
back to try the fruit, turn them over and, as they
ripened, eat them. One year the rancher lost about 150
boxes of avocadoes to the coyotes, which is roughly
5000 to 6000 pounds. This still happens to some ex-
tent, but now, after an extensive trapping campaign,
there aren't nearly as many coyotes as there used to
be. But there are infinitely more rodents. The jack-
rabbits and gophers and the like, saved from their
enemy, have flourished and populated the valley as
never before.

Frosty had all the walnuts and avocados he wanted,
so no wonder he grew fast after he came to live on the
Kelly Ranch. A lemon he tried just once; after it tied
his face in knots, he left the rest strictly alone. Oranges
he adored. Many times we saw him working on one,

intent on digging out the sections and licking the juice from the rind. The only thing he didn't like about them was that they squirted him in the face and made his hands sticky. Yet he didn't carry his oranges to water to wash them. When irrigation water was running, though, he had fingerbowls all around him. Then eating oranges was a real pleasure, and he spent a lot of time at it. We could track him by following his trail of orange peels across our grove and that of our neighbors.

I don't know whether snails are fattening, but Frosty cleaned the ranch. We had to laugh to see him out among the artichoke plants, sitting flat on his bottom, completely absorbed in scooping the snails out of their shells with one finger. A tourist eating clams on the half-shell at San Francisco's Fisherman's Wharf couldn't have enjoyed himself any more.

Added to the abundance of fruit and meat and vegetables of Frosty's diet were raw eggs. His first one he grabbed out of the egg basket we had just brought in from the chicken yard. To our horror, he immediately ran into the back bedroom with it. He just couldn't eat it on the kitchen linoleum, oh no. He had to take it under the bed, on a Persian rug! Ethel and I thought we were going to have heart attacks before we could crawl under the bed and get to him. We might as well have saved ourselves so much agony. By the time we finally reached him, he had not only nipped the egg and eaten the gooey inside, he had even eaten the shell. Furthermore, no trace of egg had he left anywhere on that precious Persian rug. Thereafter, Frosty was given as many eggs as he wanted, to be eaten wherever he liked. Never once did he make the slightest mess.

The trouble now was that he began to think other round things were eggs.

I remember well the afternoon before Christmas. Ethel and I were putting the finishing touches on the tall, stately fir tree we had set up in one corner of the living room. Earlier we had closed the doors to the animals. We wanted them to see it first when it at last stood in a glory of sparkling tinsel, ornaments, and electric lights, after we had placed the colorfully wrapped packages on the floor all around the base.

"What do you think they will do when they see the tree?" Ethel asked, straightening the star on the tip.

"Tuffy and Blackie have seen other Christmas trees in this room," I replied, plugging in the lights. "But this, of course, is Frosty's first."

"Maybe we should have a high fence of chicken wire around it."

We both laughed again. We could see Frosty climbing up that chicken wire as handily as he had the rose trellis outside the breakfast room window.

The decorating completed at last, we stood back and gazed at our handiwork. The tall fir was really a lovely sight, and its piney fragrance reminded us of our giant forest up north.

"Well," I sighed, looking at my watch, "suppose I get the odds and ends stowed away in the Fibber Magee closet while you go round up everyone. Let's have our Grand Opening now. Mom and Dad will be here in a few hours, and we have a lot yet to do."

"Fine," Ethel agreed. "Best we get our own household used to the Christmas tree before adding the confusion of more people. One thing at a time."

So Ethel went after Blackie, who was intent on a gopher hole just outside, and set her down before the tree. The big cat stared indifferently at the unaccustomed glitter, sniffed the lowest foliage, then stalked to the door and asked to be let out. Straight as an arrow, she headed back to the gopher hole. Indoor trees were strictly for humans, she told us all too plainly. To her they were unrealistic, and therefore beneath her notice.

"She doesn't know a catnip mouse is up there on that branch," Ethel said, smiling ruefully.

"She will tomorrow morning. Then perhaps the tree will take on some importance," I said. "Where's Tuffy?"

No one really had to ask. You'd have to be stone deaf not to hear his toenails raking the back screendoor. He knew something unusual was going on. As a rule, a dog senses impending festivities more quickly than a cat. Yipping happily, when Ethel admitted him, he came bounding into the living room.

The sight of a tree inside the house brought him up short. For a moment he looked up at it in great astonishment. Then, trembling with uncertainty, he skinned his eyes back and barked an experimental "Woff!" or two. Because nothing whatever happened when he did, he decided, I guess, to let the tree stay and say no more. So he contented himself with thoroughly vacuuming the floor all around it with elaborate and windy sniffs, whiffs, and snorts.

When we called Frosty, he trundled in from the poinsettia beds that lined the front lawn with their big splashes of Christmas red. No doubt he thought we had a snack for him, for he came eagerly. But as he burst into the living room he forgot about such things. There before him was a towering tree where none had been before; and unlike any he had ever seen, it was glittering with a million sparklers from base to tip. It completely overwhelmed him; it sat him back on his haunches, almost statue-still; it made his black eyes shine with colored lights as he gazed in surprise and wonder.

"Come on closer, Frosty," I said softly, "This is a

forest tree, remember? We've hung all kinds of pretty things on it because it's Christmas—and that's what we do on Christmas."

I tried to lead him toward it, but he hung back timidly—like a youngster seeing Santa Claus for the first time. Working his hands together, he scanned that tree up and then down again, taking it all in—each ornament, each colored light, each strand of popcorn, each candy cane—trying to absorb all that breathtaking beauty and brightness. The gaily wrapped boxes piled under the tree were what finally coaxed him out of his shyness and brought him closer. Trilling with pleasure, he now found the courage to reach out and touch, quickly and lightly, the tags and bows on several of the packages. Then he noticed a big, red ball hanging from the lowest limb of the tree. It was so big and so shiny he could see himself in it. For a moment he was transfixed at the sight. He didn't stay that way very long for here was an egg to end all eggs.

Suddenly Frosty recovered from his amazement. His face spread in a wide smile of Instant Bliss, and he reached for that big, red "egg". Before either of us could make a move to stop him, he had plucked the ornament from the tree and was on his way to his favorite egg-eating spot on the Persian rug, under the four-poster bed in the back room.

"No!" Ethel shouted, "Frosty—not *that!*"

"Come on quick!" I called, taking off in hot pursuit.

Considering the fact that we were both numb with weariness from a week of Christmas preparations, we made good time down the hallway. Yet Frosty was the winner by several lengths. He scooted under the bed to the farthest corner, and began to work on his prize. By the time we could crawl under and drag him out, it was too late. Most of the red ball had already disappeared.

Now we *were* in a panic, for Frosty was kicking and squirming.

"Quick—hurry—those leftover mashed potatoes in the ice box!" I said to Ethel, as we rushed into the kitchen with our problem child.

Try stuffing mashed potatoes and bread, plus a roll of cotton, down an uncomfortable and wildly resisting raccoon (already too plump with holiday snacks), if you want a hair-raising afternoon. We had it. But when dinnertime finally came, we were somehow able to stagger to the front door and smile as we greeted our guests. Behind us sat Frosty, looking extremely well and very important. After all, he had been fussed over for three solid hours without interruption, and that was an achievement any day of the week. We noticed, however, that he wasn't hungry again until Christmas was past, although nothing came of the red ball anyway, except the usual thing. He might just as well have eaten jello.

But what Frosty tried to eat the day Ethel and I went to a party and left him indoors to entertain himself certainly proves the old saying: "When the cat's away, the mice all act like rats." Left to his own devices that afternoon, Frosty experimented with a number of unknowns. For one thing, he got up on the breakfast table and unscrewed a jar of Mexican hot peppers. The hard way, he found that they weren't nearly as edible as Christmas tree ornaments.

Anyone who has had experience with these hot little demons knows what they can do. In a split second they can set your interior on fire as efficiently as if you had sprayed your mouth and throat with a flame thrower. This one must have done just that to poor Frosty, for we found it, a single piece nipped out, lying beside the jar. He had dropped it there when that first—and only—bite cauterized his tongue and mouth, and sent him scurrying in pain and fright.

After that, Frosty avoided not only the jar of Mexican hot peppers, but the breakfast table as well. Now and then he did work up courage enough to climb onto a nearby chair and look across to see if his enemy were still lurking there; then, finding that it was, he lost no time in evacuating the breakfast room. He wasn't going to be seared again.

All of this was a break for us. To our joy, we discovered that we could now leave anything—even fruit and candy—on the table, if the hot peppers were there, standing guard. It would be perfectly safe.

Not much else in the house was. At Big Basin we had done well in the little cabin. It hadn't been too large or too small for a baby coon. There weren't a lot of things he could get into. But this ten-room ranch-house, together with its acreage of fruit trees, its barn and farming equipment, was something else. Frosty was growing big and husky. He could climb, and he had a longer reach than anyone would suspect. For him, the ranch was a wonderland of things to ferret out, dismantle, and relocate. He made the most of each new opportunity as it came along. Every waking moment—both his and ours—he dedicated to a life of perpetual motion.

Ethel and I, on our way south, had set certain spring deadlines for projects to be accomplished during our sojourn at the Kelly Ranch. Yet all of these somehow merged into one, and always the same one: Frosty. No matter how many times a day we took deep breaths and started anew, we still wound up with Frosty.

For instance, just let me start typing and here he'd come on the double, although he had been happily wrestling with Tuffy out in the orange grove only moments before. At first I tried ignoring him, but that was energy wasted. He would only climb up on the windowsill, look in at me, and cry pitifully. It isn't hard to guess, I'm sure, that I got up, and let him in.

From then on he would sit nowhere but on my lap, with his back tight against my stomach. If he had just sat there and watched my flying fingers, we might have done all right, but he had to start taking a few pokes of his own at the keyboard. Before long we were playing a duet on the typewriter. Manuscripts abounded with misspelled words and peculiar punctuation that winter. Our letters were such that friends were never quite sure what we were trying to say.

Sometimes even we weren't sure, and not because Frosty was helping with the typing either. He could be in another part of the house entirely, and still scramble our thoughts so badly we couldn't reassemble and organize them. We never knew what was going to happen next. I was always hard put to get my words through the typewriter and onto paper before some crisis developed. Far too often, half-formed sentences had to be left dangling while I tried to figure out what on earth Frosty was rolling along the upper hallway toward the stairs; or why he was suddenly much too quiet.

One morning a pen full of India ink splattered all over the cartographic map I was designing for a redwood resort when a pair of heavy bookends were pushed off the table behind me. Another time, an eyebrow in a watercolor portrait streaked down and across the face and chin when, without warning, a chair in the next room was tipped over. And as long as we lived at the ranch, I never did figure out how to keep my mind on my work while little hands were slyly opening kitchen cupboards, an inch or two at a time, so that their rusty hinges kept on squealing.

About the third day that Frosty decided to play among the pots and pans inside these cupboards, I lost my temper and stomped out to the kitchen. "You cut that out!" I snapped at him, "or I'll paddle you good." He looked properly repentant, of course, and sorry, too, as he always did when reprimanded. But within moments—after I had once more become absorbed in my work—he went back to his homework with the same cupboard doors.

With growing irritation I gathered together my drawing board, the ink, and the pens, and moved to the table in the breakfast room. From there I had a clear view of the kitchen. "This," I thought quaintly, "will fix that monkey-business."

I don't know whatever gave me such an idea.

As soon as my attention accidentally wandered back to my work, Frosty began to ease open the cupboard doors again. This time I put my pen down, turned my head slowly in his direction, and impaled him with the long, sharp point of my most ferocious, bald-eagle glare. It stopped him, all right. Jerking his hand away from the cupboard doorknob, as if he'd just touched a red-hot stove, he sat back and beamed with his most fetching "Who, me?" look. His halo had never shone more brightly.

Gritting my teeth, I went back to my pen-and-ink drawing. But not for long. Out of the corner of my eye I could see Frosty watching me—and at the same time moving his hand closer and closer to the cupboard doorknob.

This was the moment my patience disintegrated. I must have had a deadly gleam in my eyes as I charged into the kitchen, because Frosty retreated before so much fury. He rolled himself back into the nearest corner, the flat top of his head down on the linoleum. Slowly he raised his rump and ringed tail and got ready for his paddling. He did everything but pick a switch off a tree and hand it to me. Furthermore, his black eyes were shining, and that big (and adorable, darn it) smile spread from ear to ear. Now how do you go about punishing such an imp?

Don't ever doubt it—he was counting on my asking myself that very question.

Often when Ethel and I had all the rugged individualism from Frosty that we could bear for one day, we banished him from the house. He didn't like this, because he preferred to make his own decisions. So he found ways of getting around us. The most successful was to climb up on a window ledge close to one of us and sit there, crying as if his heart would break. We could understand that his heart was broken temporarily. We also saw that it healed lightning-fast after we gave up and let him in. At those kiss-and-make-up times, he would rush to us with all the love and fervor of one who is being reunited with long-lost dear ones. Quickly he'd forgive us our mistakes, and never seemed to hold them against us.

Try as we might, I think we were able to outwit Frosty with only one trick. Accidentally we found a way to get him downstairs when we wanted him. Considering the fact that he had adopted the upper floor and its balcony as his own private domain, we felt more than a little elated over our discovery.

We hadn't been at the ranch more than a week when, suddenly, here was the solution to our problem. No longer would we have to climb the stairs and fish him out of the bathroom or any one of several closets. Now, all we had to do was to step into the downstairs bathroom and flush the toilet. It would bring him every time, and in a hurry, too. Down the steps he'd rumble. At the bottom he'd skid around the corner, rush along the hallway, make a scrambled right turn, slide across the linoleum to the toilet—and jump in. Perhaps I'd better say he'd reach in, for he was now too big to ever dive through the white oval again.

But a slight thing like outgrowing his babbling brook didn't stop Frosty. He just acted as if nothing had happened, and turned it into a paddling pool. He even transferred some of his devotion to the bathtub. In fact, he invented a game that included both.

First our coon would turn on one of the tub's faucets, and ram a finger up it so that the water sprayed all directions—especially into his face. Then, after so many sneezes and snorts, he'd carry the stopper to the toilet, where he dabbled it in the water for a few minutes before returning it to the tub; then, hopping back to the toilet, he'd flush it, jump back to the tub, and spray water once more. He never did the flushing with the stopper in the toilet; I suspect it was because he didn't want to lose his toy down the hole.

We didn't worry about why he always insisted on this entire routine. He had his reasons, and he was entitled to them. There was one thing we did learn, however: either we stayed until he had finished, or he would head for the upper floor. His threat worked. We stayed. But the wait was worth it, for there was no more struggling with Frosty upstairs. All we had to do now was zip up our patience until he had gone through his act. After that we were free to run for the kitchen to find out how badly our dinner had burned.

While all these things were going on, Tuffy was never far away, cheering as only a doggie can—by yipping hysterically, and panting with approval until his tongue hung halfway to the floor. He thought Frosty was the most wonderful, the most exciting, the most entertaining pal possible. He was Frosty's Public, his publicity agent, his Yes Man from morning until night. But after the sun went down and he had eaten, he was only a tired Scottie. From then on, he was concerned solely with his own comfort. This was the hour when he chose to make a ceremony of digesting his dinner.

This simple rite always started out well enough. Heaving a big sigh of contentment, Tuffy would sprawl full length on the front room rug and close his eyes. Not long afterward Frosty would wander in and lie down companionably with his head on the dog's flank. For a time Ethel and I could keep our minds on what we were reading, although we both knew that this pleasant state of affairs wasn't going to last long. We would notice that Frosty's eyes were tightly shut; on his face, the look of one about to count his blessings. But we weren't deceived.

Within a matter of minutes he would have opened one eye far enough to see how to reach over and tinkle the bell on Tuffy's collar. That awakened the Scottie, of course, and to be awakened annoyed him. Trying hard to ignore the teasing, he made a little distant thunder deep in his throat, and once more sank into sleep.

That solved nothing whatever, for the bell would tinkle again—and again and again and again. Finally, rousing with a jerk, Tuffy would peel back his eyes and woof once or twice in more vigorous protest. This always prompted Frosty to roll over—away from the noisy, toothy end of the dog—so that he now lay facing the tail. Relieved of annoyance, Tuffy settled down once more and soon began to snore. Frosty waited for that, eyes open and twinkling with deviltry. When he decided that his friend was now peacefully asleep, he'd reach furtively under the dog's belly with fingers just probing enough to blast any dreams to smithereens.

You'd scold Frosty? Not much use. He'd sit there and take it like a trouper, both hands covering his eyes to shut out the awful sight of you in your more unlove-ly moments. And as soon as you stopped speaking, he'd

move one finger just a tiny bit so he could peek out and
see if it was safe to carry on from there. After he was
sure that the storm had passed, he'd drop his hands
from his face, and the scolding from his mind, as
instantly and utterly as if he had flipped a switch.

To preserve Tuffy's sanity, as well as his rights as
Master of the Ranch, we'd finally have to show our
coon to his bed in the back room—and that failing, the
big, black out-of-doors. He didn't care. More and
more, as we moved into January, Frosty was coming
to love the night.

13

WHEN YOU'RE RAISING a wild animal, word soon gets around. They are a great curiosity to most people. We had a good many visitors that winter at the Kelly Ranch, although they didn't come in droves as they had at Big Basin, when Frosty was small. Now that he was almost fully grown, not everyone was anxious to tangle with him. Twenty-two pounds of raccoon can seem nothing short of mountainous when he's bounding toward you—even if all he wants is to smother you with affection and sunshine. Some of our friends shriveled up into tight little knots as Frosty, throttle wide open and eyes shining merrily, rushed forward to welcome them and lay his heart at their feet.

Besides the people who came to the ranch knowing they'd find a coon there were those who came expecting to find only Ethel and me, Tuffy and Blackie. They had my sympathy.

I remember the mechanic, Mr. McFee, who drove in one evening just before dark to find out what was wrong with the tractor. He fiddled with it for a few minutes, decided what tools he'd need to bring to work on it next day, and then got into his car to leave. While sitting there, thinking over his diagnosis, he took a pack of cigarettes out of his shirt pocket and prepared to light up. But he didn't get quite that far.

Suddenly, and without any warning, something big and furry flew from the back seat and landed on his shoulders and neck with all the delicacy of a rampaging gorilla. Strong arms reached down his front and snatched the cigarette out of his mouth and the pack out of his hand. For a few moments he must have been paralyzed with surprise and fright. Then, shouting at the top of his lungs, he leaped out of his car, ricocheted around the back yard, and burst in through the back door of the ranchhouse.

"Something's—something's—loose!" he gasped, barely able to speak at all. "It's a hairy ape! He's wild! He—he grabbed me. Get the police!" There wasn't enough breath left in him to say more, so he stomped around the kitchen, swinging his arms in wide circles fighting to regain his breath.

Even though it was instantly apparent to us what had happened out there in the dark, we shouldn't have laughed. But we did, we couldn't help ourselves.

"What's funny?" Mr. McFee bellowed, understandably affronted at our thoughtlessness.

"Nothing really," Ethel admitted. "But don't worry. You're safe. I think you met our coon."

"Coon? *Coon?*"

"Yes—we have a raccoon."

"He tried to strangle me."

"No," I said, "he's never hurt anything in his life. Come on, let's go out; we'll show you. He's a pet. You'll love him."

"Love him?" the mechanic roared, his face purpling.

"He's just a little coon," I said, knowing better than that, and crossing my fingers because I did. "He was only trying to get acquainted with you." (This, at least, was true, I told myself.)

Mr. McFee gave me a blistering look that, by all rights, should have shriveled me where I stood. Yet it didn't; rather, it made me want more than ever to prove to this unbeliever what a darling Frosty actually was.

"Come on," I repeated. "Let me show you."

Taking a flashlight off the table, and snapping on the yard light as I went out the screendoor, I led our doubting visitor to his car.

As I had predicted, there on the seat was Frosty, looking up at us with an irresistible ear-to-ear smile spreading across his masked face. Between his hands was a cigarette, and he was rolling it back and forth, back and forth. All around him, scattered over the seat and floor, lay the rest of the pack. They had already been rolled, and were in various stages of advanced ruin.

"So that's it," I laughed, opening the car door. "You had cigarettes on you. He adores them—just to roll like that. It's the feel of them in the palms of his hands."

"No foolin'!" Wonder was beginning to replace anger now.

Slowly I pulled Frosty toward me until I could pick him up. This was easy to do because the last cigarette was just then disintegrating, and was therefore no more interest to him. Besides, here was a brand new audience to wow.

I took his hands in mine and turned their palms up. All this time he was studying the stranger's face intently.

"See—a raccoon's hands are pretty much like ours," I said. "No thumb, but five fingers and bare palms. And they can do almost anything ours can. Feel how soft they are." Cautiously Mr. McFee extended an index finger and made himself touch one of Frosty's palms. As he did so, his finger was encircled ever so gently—as if a baby had taken hold of it, and was gripping it in its fist. Ethel winked at me over Mr. McFee's shoulder as we heard him gasp with surprise.

"They ARE soft," he conceded reluctantly.

"And notice the creases in them—like in our own hands."

"His hind feet, too."

"That's right. In dust or mud they leave the same kind of impressions the hands and feet of a human baby do. Many a person who didn't know this has been fooled—even a new ranger once."

"You don't say." The man was warming to the subject now. All fear and anger gone, his heart was melting fast.

I went on: "Coon hands can remove jar lids, undo latches, turn knobs, push windows open, take corks out of bottles—all kinds of things."

"Honest?"

I nodded. "Wouldn't you like to hold Frosty, Mr. McFee?" For Frosty had stretched out his arms to him, and how in the world could anyone resist such unqualified acceptance as that? Mr. McFee didn't try. He just took Frosty from me—albeit awkwardly and with some hesitation, because he'd never touched a live wild animal before.

But Frosty, with his usual gay abandon, immediately went to work making himself at home in our visitor's arms. Eagerly—and clear up to the elbows—he reached both hands inside his new friend's shirt front and kneaded his smooth, warm stomach—and ribs, too, I'm afraid, until Mr. McFee was so convulsed that he almost doubled up: another one of those ticklish people that the world seems to be so full of.

Nevertheless, Frosty thought he was wonderful. I suspect this husky man with the deep voice and strong arms reminded him of the park rangers he used to know. Anyway, before the mechanic left the ranch that night, Frosty had adopted him as a bosom friend.

Next day, when Mr. McFee returned to fix the tractor, he didn't have to put in long, dull, greasy hours working alone. He had an assistant, and for free. The only thing, Frosty was what you might call Unskilled Labor. He knew little about tractors except that they were fun to climb around over, and great to ride upon when they were rumbling down the grove between the rows of citrus trees. Helping to take one down, put in a new part, and get it all back together again was, of course, something out of the ordinary. But let it never be said he didn't try.

Every gear, nut, and bolt the mechanic took out, and laid on a small canvas, Frosty picked up and inspected. And he didn't always think to put it back in the same place. But Mr. McFee didn't care too much. To him, all of this was plain amazing and terribly funny. We could hear him laughing as he pointed out the mechanical failure, and the reason for it, and explained, so even I could understand, what he was going to do by way of repair. I know because I watched from the corner of the barn twice that morning. I could hear everything that was being said, although all I could see of Mr. McFee was greasy jeans and a red bandana hanging out of his hip pocket. And all I could see of Frosty, standing on the treads, was his rump and ringed tail pointing skyward. The rest of him was down deep in the tractor's interior somewhere, where deft hands were at work.

Even this idyll had to end—as companionable as it was. The moment came when a tractor part, laid to one side for special attention, left the scene abruptly. On furry legs it went galloping out into the orange grove to one of the irrigation furrows, there to be washed and examined minutely. Behind it, at some distance and yelling for a prompt return, came the man responsible for its welfare. He wasn't angry, not a bit; the truth of it was, he was enjoying this little break. At several dollars an hour, he could afford to.

In order that the Kelly tractor be repaired and ready for service in our time, I had to step in. "Come on," I whispered to Frosty, as I knelt down beside him there at the furrow. "This isn't any fun; and I have a *marvelous* idea."

If I had said "horrible" instead of "marvelous", I'm reasonably sure he wouldn't have known the difference. It was just that I seemed excited and thrilled, and he knew from past experience that when I sounded that way, I always had something special to share with him.

Straightaway, the bearing or gasket or whatever it was dropped kerplunk in the mud and was forgotten as he gave me his full attention.

"Tell you what let's do," I proposed. "Let's go into the barn and clean our hands. Then let's you and I sneak off into the house. I'm going to show you how to play the piano."

And that's exactly what we did. Trundling along beside me, and talking a blue streak all the way, Frosty was a willing collaborator—and a fine piano student, too. Together we sat on the bench and played different tunes in duet. He found the keys pleasant to touch, and the fact that they made a pretty sound when pressed utterly absorbed him the rest of the afternoon. I spoiled a beautiful friendship that day, but ranching on the Kelly place once again went forward.

So also did another of my deadlines—forward toward the summer.

Other people would be coming to the Kelly ranch from time to time. Frosty wasn't going to lack for new friends. But the welder who came to do some work in the ranch shop was not one of them. This man either had no love for animals, or else no sense of humor. Or perhaps welding is touchy business.

Anyway, a few days after the mechanic left, Frosty discovered this fellow out in the shop, busy at whatever welders do. Naturally he was curious about him. Not only had he never seen him before, he had never beheld one of those fiery monsters the man gripped in one hand. For a long time Frosty hung around the workbench, watching the strange goings-on. He was quiet about it. Probably the heat and awesome roar of the welder's torch dazzled him at first.

But by and by Frosty had to make his presence felt. This man and his fire-breathing accomplice were ignoring him. He had to do something about that, so he circled at a safe distance, trying to figure out a way. As always, it came to him. From a nearby tool shelf he reached over and ran his hand up the welder's rolled sleeve—merely to feel his soft skin and establish friendly relations.

I know nothing about welding, but I should think a move of this kind, when you're leaning over a work bench, playing white hot fire on a metal part, could be disastrous—even if it is prompted by the best of intentions. As it was, its violent effect on the welder's tensions was disaster enough. Like a tightly wound spring, suddenly released, the man spun around, shoved his goggles onto the top of his head, and glared. "Gad!" he exploded.

Frosty recoiled before so much venom. Instinct told him that here was a man to whom coons were no joy, for in him they stirred no pleasant memories, unless they were those of a coonskin cap. Moreover, he seemed to have none of the gaiety of spirit or warmth of heart of Frosty's other friends. One of the farm hands, who happened to be in the shop that day and saw it all, told us later that when the man turned on Frosty, the coon hurriedly backed off into a corner, talking to himself, and playing nervously with his hands. He didn't know what to do with this new kind of human.

Characteristically he lost no time in deciding. After the welder once more bent over his work, Frosty climbed a short ladder back of him and sat down on one of the steps. There, in the next few minutes, he contrived a way to get back at this hostile stranger. Holding onto the ladder upright with one hand, he stretched out with the other—far enough to grab the welder's shirt. Then, with a mighty jerk, he yanked his shirttail out of his pants.

From my typewriter in the den I heard the rising crescendo of angry yelling and what sounded like hammers and hatchets bouncing off the sides of the barn. I set out for the shop on a dead run—and a good thing I did, too. As it happened, I got there at the precise moment human endurance had reached its shaking limits.

"Get that brat out of here!" the man screamed at me, brandishing a Stillson wrench. "Get him out of here before I weld his infernal hands to his belly!"

The prudent thing to do seemed to be to retreat, and fast, so I carried Frosty to the house and locked him in the back screenporch.

At my typewriter again, I tried to collect my thoughts and complete the chapter I'd been working on for many days. But when you have a raccoon confined against his will in the same house, creative writing turns into a broken record: you repeat yourself over and over again, participles dangle, infinitives are split, modifiers crop up in the funniest places.

Just then I was struggling for sentence variety. "Struggling" was the word, all right, for I could hear Frosty out there on the back porch, restlessly pacing, poking into everything in search of something different to engage his interest. As usual, he managed to find it, although he didn't get to enjoy it very long. This time it was Ethel who put a crimp in his plans. Returning from the mailbox, she went to the back porch to finish the laundry she had put to soak earlier, and discovered him.

He was sitting on the counter beside the tub, reaching down into her washing with both hands. Because the sheets had billowed high among the soapsuds, as they often do when air is trapped in them, these ballooning pillows had become the objects of his affection. He was finding them exquisitely soft to pat. And every time he patted them, they squished and foamed and sprang back into the round, ready for him to pat some more.

This would have been fine had Frosty's hands been

clean; they would have helped Ethel with the washing. But after the shirttail yanking, Frosty had puddled briefly in some spilled smudgepot oil he'd found in that dark corner of the shop to which he'd fled for security reasons. At this moment he was up to his shoulders in suds, having the time of his life handblockprinting both sheets and pillow cases. And he was so absorbed in originating a distinctive all-over pattern of black on white that he didn't hear Ethel rushing toward him. He didn't know she was anywhere near until, without any warning, he was seized from behind. Then he reacted the way any wild animal, and most domesticated ones, usually do under such circumstances. He turned around in his skin—something a coon is adept at—and bit her. He drew two little beads of red on her index finger.

That was the first time Frosty had ever nipped either of us, and it taught us a lesson: you never grab a wild animal from the rear unless you don't mind if he engraves his mark somewhere in your hide; rather, you approach calmly from the front, so he can see you and judge your intent; you clench your teeth, making it virtually impossible to yell at him, and consequently throw everything into an uproar; furthermore, you make sure to smile and be gentle-voiced and turn your hands upward. No one can strike with his palms up— something animal intelligence is well aware of.

Frosty's was, of course. Besides, he didn't have any reason to think that either of us would come along and hit him for his misdeeds. We never had. Paddling him was energy wasted. We rarely used force, even to snatch him to safety from the most precarious situations. No matter what he'd been dabbling his hands in—a bowl of whipped cream, the garbage disposal, Ethel's Chanel No. 5, the jar of ant paste, or the two dozen glasses of freshly made marmalade cooling on the drainboard—we always tried to go at him head on: "easy does it."

The Day of the Biting at the Washtubs Ethel had acted before she thought. She never did that again.

By the time I appeared on the back porch in answer to her summons, Frosty had already gone back to his artwork. Typical of coons everywhere, his hands were busy with one thing, his eyes with something else entirely. Through the screen he had spied a pair of linnets flitting among the bamboo. So while his hands block printed the sheets in the tub, his eyes sparkled merrily at the antics of the birds outside. The biting incident was as gone from his mind as if it had never occurred.

"This was my fault," Ethel explained ruefully, showing me the toothmarks just above her fingernail. "But for goodness sakes, take Frosty out of here or we'll never get these sheets clean."

I thought a minute; then, trying to get his attention, I said in my most persuasive voice, "Frosty, how about a frog hunt in the barranca?" With that I gave him a wink and a vigorous "Come-on-let's-go" sign. Since my tone of voice suggested something jolly and carefree— and a wee bit mysterious—it drew Frosty out of his reverie. In an instant he was at my heels, eager for new and exciting adventure.

Together we crossed the orange grove toward the long row of eucalyptus trees, leaving Ethel free to go find the mercurochrome and finish the washing.

Me? I wound up helping Frosty hunt frogs down in the bottom of the damp barranca. That's the way half my deadlines were met that winter.

And the sheets? Frosty did such a good job on them that several years afterwards, when they were worn out and had to be replaced, the dark handprints were still there—even to the natural creases and wrinkles.

14

THE MORNING FROSTY put the prints there, neither Ethel nor I were in a very good humor. Those sheets had been some of our best. Now they were anything but that, for how could we use them for company? Hanging out on the clothesline to dry, snow white except for the many little handprints, they attracted a lot of raucous attention. They sent the Mexican-American ranch hands into gales of laughter. The men knew our coon only too well. He insisted on helping them with their chores when they really didn't need— or want—his help.

Later in the day, as we folded the sheets and put them on the hall shelves, we were to look more tolerantly—even fondly—on those black handprints. Sometimes the events of only a few minutes can change a person's whole attitude about a thing. That afternoon ours was to change so that never again would we grouse about our personalized linens.

Soon after lunch our phone rang. A woman in town, whom I didn't know, was calling. "We hear you have a pet raccoon," she said. "So have we. That is, we'd like to make a pet of him, but he doesn't seem to want to be one."

"What appears to be the trouble?" I asked.

"I don't know," was the answer, "But he keeps growling whenever we come near. He won't eat either, and we've offered him everything we can think of."

"Where did you get him?" I queried further.

"Down in the riverbottom. My husband brought him home a few days ago."

"Do you have him caged?" I asked.

"Yes," the woman replied, "but we have to. He acts like he'd tear us to pieces. Would you mind coming to see him and tell us what's the matter? We want a coon pet. We can't see why he won't be one."

"I'll be over," I answered, and hung up. Turning to Ethel I fumed, "How do people expect a coon to love them if he's caged and miserable?"

I had no idea how miserable that coon was until I saw him.

Following the woman, her husband, and their three boys out behind their garage, I knelt down beside the small cage that was swarming with flies. There, inside, among a scattering of decaying food of all kinds, crouched the half-grown coon these people expected to make into a pet.

"He just won't be friendly," the woman complained.

"He's not a bit gentle," the man added truthfully. The boys stood to one side, silently waiting to hear what I was going to say.

For once in my life words nearly failed me. Horrified beyond speech, I found myself looking at a poor creature whose hands were crushed and bloody. He was shaking with what must have been nearly unbearable pain, and as he backed away from me, he bared his teeth and snarled. Then he glanced at the others, and snarled some more. His eyes were glassy with fever.

I gasped with shock at what I saw. "Whatever happened to this wretched coon?" I asked, thinking they had found him and were trying to nurse him back to health.

"It's his hands," one of the boys blurted. "But he don't tame none. We're trying to feed him so he'll get well."

"But what's happened to his hands?" I asked again, feeling sick at my stomach.

"Well, we catched him because we've always wanted one for a pet," the man explained. "But this one's no good. Why won't he tame?"

I could feel the fires of fury rising in me as I got to my feet. My skin was starting to prickle, and there was a pounding in my ears. Beads of perspiration had already formed on my forehead. It took me a few long minutes to be able to ask my question, fearing what awful thing I might do when I heard the answer that would surely come.

"Did *you* set a steel trap for this raccoon?" I demanded, trying to keep my voice steady.

"Why yes," the man said, "How else you goin' to get a coon pet?"

On my way home I stopped at the house of the Humane Society officer. There was only one way for that poor coon to find peace, and that was the officer's duty. All the explaining in the world about steel traps and what they do to living things wouldn't have made the slightest impression on those people. They had expected to make a loving pet of an animal whose hands they had deliberately and willfully mangled to a bloody pulp. A shot mercifully released the suffering prisoner from a fate worse than death.

Back at the ranch that evening, I sat before the fire while Frosty mussed my hair, ran his fingers around in the inner recesses of my ears, and reached inside my dress front and felt of my skin all he wanted. I never objected once when he turned pages of my book that I wasn't ready to have turned. Somehow it didn't seem to be very important when he pulled the bristles out of my hair brush, and spent most of an hour taking the alarm clock apart. Or perhaps I'd better say that another way: it *was* important, for he had hands to do it with—soft, warm, incredibly sensitive hands that were whole. They were his eyes, his life.

Frosty may have sensed my feelings that night, for bursting with the joy of living and being loved, he went all out to keep the family in turmoil. When at last all of us were weary from it, we gave up and went to bed.

As usual, Frosty climbed into the big, four-poster bed with me; and I was glad, for this was one of those cold nights when the smudge pots in the groves would have to be lighted. Snuggling against my back, Frosty heaved a long, quavering sigh of contentment, and as quickly as he did everything else, settled comfortably into his dreams. It was then I noticed for the first time that Frosty, stretched out full length, now completely covered my back. He was getting to be a big coon.

15

ONE DAY SHORTLY after the beginning of the new year, Roger Kelly came in from furrowing out the lemon grove and sank into an easy chair to rest. "Well," he sighed, "this is some rainy season we're having. So far we've received only 3.75 inches. Everything's sure dry."

"What do you suppose has happened to our usual winter downpour?"

"Search me. The rains just don't seem to be able to make it over the Tehachapis. A storm front starts south all right; whopping black clouds sit down on the mountains, and you'd swear we were all going to be washed into the ocean. Then boom! The darned Santa Ana

winds start howling in off the desert and the thunder-
heads get blown right back where they came from."

"I'll be glad when the wind stops," I said. "My hair's
been standing on end for a week now."

"We hardly dare touch the animals," Ethel put in.
"Electricity jumps onto them from our fingertips. Poor
Tuffy ran from me this morning—I think I nearly
electrocuted him."

Roger smiled and lit up his pipe. "One good thing
about the east wind, though—we don't have to smudge
when it's blowing. Haven't had to fire in ten days now.
Boy, I hate that getting out in the middle of the night,
when it's so still and cold. I like my sleep."

"Do you think you'll need to smudge any more this
winter?"

"Probably. February is going to be cold, they say.
Anyway, we've got the pots filled and ready again.
Good crew lined up. But usually after one of these east
winds, it's nice and mild for a while."

"Yes," I said, "and that will be just fine with me. I'll
enjoy a spell without either wind or smudge."

Ethel added, "I'm going to be real happy when we
no longer have to get up looking like end men in a
minstrel show." We all laughed, although it wasn't
funny. Many a night during the winter months temperatures dipped down into the twenties. When the ther-
mometer dropped to 28 degrees, the pots in the lemon
groves had to be lighted to keep the fruit from freezing; when it dropped a little further—to 26 degrees—
the pots in the orange groves had to be fired.

Sometimes this became necessary early in the evening, at eight or nine o'clock. But even when it didn't,
when the firing was delayed until after midnight, there
was always a heavy, blue-black pall of oily smoke hanging low over the valley for several hours after sunup.
No wonder we got up looking as if we had been

blackfaced; no wonder light-colored curtains and linens soon became dingy; white animals, grey; grey ones, black. On Tuffy and Blackie, already brunette, we couldn't see any oily film, although when we petted them we found it was there. Frosty turned a shade or two darker after a smudgy night, so we always swabbed off his white trim in order that he could look more like himself. He enjoyed this. After all, it was special attention and devotion he was receiving. He had a strong affinity for both.

Rested now, Roger got up and stretched. "Time to get back to my cultivating," he said, heading for the back door. "I think the wind's dying down. When it quits I believe I'll have the house painted. Sort of a surprise for Mom and Dad when they come home."

"If you have to smudge some more, won't that mess up your paint job?" I asked.

"Don't think so. If it does, the rain will wash it off. At least I *hope* we'll eventually get rain. We'd better— and soon. For one thing, I'd like not to have to irrigate again until spring."

"Frosty will be sorry if you don't."

Roger threw back his head and laughed heartily. He and Frosty were great pals. "Well, we shall see. Meanwhile, I'll arrange for the paint job. I'm going to call Butch Barnes today. Maybe he can come out the first quiet day we have. Capable fellow. Knows his painting."

"We'll watch for him," I said.

The day Butch Barnes arrived with all his brushes and buckets and ladders was a red-letter day for Frosty, for here was something different going on, someone new to win. He entered into the spirit of the house-painting with all the enthusiasm of a fisherman who has just discovered a stream swarming with trout. Moreover, for Frosty and Butch, it was love at first sight. That entire week they were inseparable—actually inseparable.

Hardly an hour passed that the coon wasn't plastered on the painter's broad back, his arms around the man's neck, his feet hooked into his belt. All day long they went up and down the ladder that way. Before the week was over, the fellow's shoulder muscles must have become Herculean. But he not only didn't mind taking a piggybank supervisor up and down with him, he loved it. So did Frosty. His happy smile clouded only when he couldn't get hold of the spray gun. However, the painter did explain to him why this had to be. "You don't have a union card, my friend," he told him, "so you can't do any of the work."

Frosty must have accepted his explanations, for after several of them he seemed content merely to lean over the man's shoulder and stamp his hand prints here and there on the building.

All of this was hard on Tuffy. Every time he wanted to play with his pal, he found Frosty was up in the air somewhere. So he had to be satisfied with sniffing the buckets of paint and the ladder and the painter, when he came down. For a few days the dog was a desolate soul. He just wasn't made on the same floor plan as Frosty. Nature hadn't intended him to climb onto a man's back and ride up and down on a ladder. Completely earthbound, the best he could do was stand below and whine with envy and frustration, although he did rush noisily upstairs and out on the balcony when operations reached that level. Still, he felt deserted and left out. We felt sorry for him.

"I'm going to town after a bone or two for Tuffy," Ethel announced one afternoon. "No one should have to be that miserable."

When the paint job was completed at last, Mr. Barnes, in a gesture of undying friendship, gave Frosty something to remember him by. You might say it was his autograph, for before he cleaned his equipment and went home, he sprayed a little creme-colored paint on the coon's rump. Many were the times afterwards that either Ethel or I would say, "There'll never be any question about recognizing Frosty, whether he'd remember us or not." That spot of creme-colored fur on his left hip was going to be there for some time. Now what other coon in Southern California would be so lovingly decorated?

Riding up and down on a ladder all week made a lasting impression on Frosty. After his stint as a painter's helper was over, he climbed everyone he could find. He was even to climb the special ladder Roger made at his own ranch, and brought down one morning. It rose high above the truckbed to which it was attached, and on the top was a crow's-nest big enough to hold a man. From here, next fall, a ranch worker with a pole would shake the nuts out of the upper branches of the walnut trees as another worker drove the truck down between the rows.

"That's quite a thing," I said gazing up at it in wonder.

"Thanks," Roger said, pleased by the compliment. "It'll help us get the crop in faster, that's for sure. It's not finished yet, though. Have to brace it with more steel before it can be used. Is it okay if David and Linda stay here and play with Frosty while I go to town to the sheet metal shop?"

David and Linda, Roger's young son and daughter, were just then coming down the driveway from gathering some poinsettias to take home to their mother.

"Is it all right if we stay, Daddy?" Linda called.

"You just know it is, Linda," I called back. "You're always welcome here, you two. Ethel loves to have you come; so do I; and so does Frosty."

As the boy and girl came around the corner of the house, Frosty heard them and threw himself against the back screendoor so that he literally exploded into the yard.

"Let me take your poinsettias," I said, reaching for them. "I'll dip their stems in boiling water and put them in a vase or something, while you and David try to outthink Frosty. Here he is, and really glad to see you. Over by the sprinkler, David, you'll find his stuffed gunny sack, if you want it."

This was just the kind of an arrangement Frosty loved—one where he could be the center of attention, and the main reason for the gathering of people. He knew he was It when Linda giggled and giggled at him while he took everything out of her purse and inspected it. He knew it when David burst into gales of laughter over having his stomach skin kneaded as if it were a biscuit. An audience that thought everything he did wonderful, always brought out the best in Frosty—or perhaps I should say The Most. And that day it was The Most.

For an hour or two he tried all of his tricks, and played all of his games. He let the youngsters maul him; he chewed on them gently while acting as fierce as a cornered bear. Generally he saw to it that his guests had a good, vigorous time. Quite a hunk of coon by now, he eventually wore out David and Linda with his roughhouse—but not before he had covered himself with glory. In the process of dragging a pair of old overalls out of the shop and toward the walnut grove, he discovered Roger's truck and unfinished ladder tower.

For a moment he eyed it in surprise. Where had this thing come from? He hadn't seen it before. As the youngsters squealed with delight, he climbed aboard and clambered hand over hand up the rungs of the ladder. Linda was entranced. Running to the house she called to us, "Come out! Please come out and see what Frosty's doing now. He's climbing Daddy's ladder tower. He's going way up!"

You might know Ethel and I would drop everything to go and watch Frosty shine. He could count on us for that. He had always counted on us to bail him out of situations he couldn't quite handle, too. By the time Linda, Ethel, and I got to the ladder tower truck, Frosty needed bailing out.

Showing off with all the ham of an old-time vaudeville hoofer, our little coon had climbed to the top. There he encountered the ladder's last rung. It was different from the others. It was a wide, flat piece of metal, bolted to the side of the crow's nest in such a way that Frosty was unable to secure any kind of a tight grip on it, although he kept trying. David, unaware of Frosty's problem, was all boyish energy and enthusiasm. "I'm going up, too," he announced hoisting himself onto the truck bed.

"Wait, David," I warned. "Your father told me the tower isn't finished yet. It isn't ready to take much weight. He went to town, you know, to buy steel bracing parts." Disappointed, the lad dropped back to the ground. Together all three of us shaded our eyes so that we could watch Frosty high on the ladder.

Without any question something was wrong up there. Balked by that last rung, Frosty began to look down at us as if he were uncertain what to do next. Then his hind feet slipped off the rung he had been standing on. For a moment or two he hung by his hands, thrashing around for support.

"What do you suppose is the trouble?" Ethel whispered to me, not wanting to alarm the children.

"I don't know," I answered, "but I think he's tired. He's been wrestling, and climbing things all morning.

'Get your feet on a rung, Frosty!' I shouted up to him.
'Get your feet on a rung!' "

But that was something Frosty couldn't seem to do.
We could tell that his arms were quivery-tired and that
for once he was frightened. Plaintively he began to cry
and looked down at us for help. There was no bravado
or smarty in him now. He was on the verge of panic,
for here we were, far, far below him; and not a one of
us was making any move to come to his rescue, as we
always had when he was in a jam. This time there
wasn't a thing we could do to help him.

Still thinking Frosty was clowning especially for our
benefit, David and Linda cheered him on, shouting
advice as happily as they had wrestled with him on the
lawn earlier that morning.

"What are we going to do?" Ethel whispered.

"I don't know," I answered. "There isn't anything
we can do except try to catch him if he falls. And if we
can't—" There was no use saying it. We both knew
such a fall would probably injure him badly, perhaps
even kill him. Both of us scrambled up onto the truck
bed. We knew we had to be ready to catch him.

"Get your feet on that rung!" David called to the
coon again, beginning to realize now that Frosty was
not fooling. "Get your feet on that rung, boy!"

In another moment—and in the nick of time—he
did. Disaster seemed to have been diverted. But not
quite. Frosty was still crying, looking down at us. His
arms just didn't have the strength left to respond to his
will to go up or down.

"Stay and rest a minute!" I called up to him, gripping the ladder with both my hands, more to give him
courage than anything else. Oh, if his arms would just
hold out for a little while longer, until we could think
of something to do. Once again Frosty whimpered and
looked down helplessly. Once again he appeared to be

nearly paralyzed with exhaustion. We were running out of time.

As Ethel and I frantically tried to figure out a way to rescue our coon, we saw him begin to inch his way toward one of the ladder's long uprights. Shaking with the effort, he placed the flat top of his head against it, and pushed steadily. Carefully—very, *very* carefully—his rear end backed away toward the other upright, found it, and pressed against it tightly. Moving more gingerly than he had in his life before, he managed to stretch his spine so that, purely with his own muscle power, he was able to brace himself between the two sides of the ladder. The top of his head was against one, his rump, against the other. When he felt himself to be secure, for the moment at least, he let go with one hand, then the other. He just let them hang and rest.

For a full two minutes Frosty, with his own strength and will power, wedged himself across the top of that ladder, dangling his arms loosely until they had rested, and their strength and circulation had been restored. Then once again, moving slowly and very, *very* carefully, he righted himself, took hold of the rungs, and descended the ladder to the bottom. By this time David and Linda had caught onto what he was doing and, with admiration for his courage and cool thinking, went all out to make a big fuss over him.

"Say," David exclaimed, as our coon dropped off the bottom rung onto the flat bed of the truck, "that was using your head for sure."

"And your rump, too," Linda reminded him.

"Come here, you little bum. Don't you know coons don't pole walnuts?"

"David, he wanted a high lookout station where he could oversee the whole ranch, all at once."

"Yes, but Frosty, you should have checked with us first to see if it was safe."

"Anyhow, that was a very smart thing to have done, Frosty. You are a brave coon."

"Do you think he really knew he was in danger?" David asked, turning to us.

"He sure did," I assured him.

"And he figured out how to save himself," Linda marveled, eyes glowing. "Come here, you little darling. And she wrapped her arms around Frosty and hugged him.

Frosty had been a clown when he scrambled to the top of that ladder; he was a hero when he came down—and not only to two thrilled and excited kids, but to Ethel and me as well. At that moment no one could have persuaded us that there was another animal in the world as smart as a raccoon. I'll always agree with the experts that there aren't many.

As Frosty let us rub his hands and arms, he must have read our thoughts and felt our enormous relief. By now he was also beginning to get his second wind, and with it that comfortable, secure feeling one has when, after a close call, he is safe at last.

Then embarrassment set in. Frosty began to suffer acutely from a fracture of pride. He began to feel foolish. This meant that he must do something devastatingly spectacular to prove that the escapade on the ladder was no accident; that, on the contrary, it was a little something extra he had thrown in especially for the delight and amazement of our young visitors. With a flourish, he jumped down off the truck and took off toward the lemon grove in search of bigger and better projects. Right after him, shouting with pleasure, ran Linda and David.

Ethel and I watched them disappear in the trees, and then turned toward the house and some dishwashing, wishing we could indulge in the luxury of a nervous breakdown. We were all in. "Whew," I breathed, "maybe today would be a good time to go down to Los Angeles, sit on the corner of Seventh and relax This country life with a coon is getting to be too much for my old age."

"Mine, too," Ethel replied, "but at last we know there's nothing else on the ranch now that Frosty hasn't seen, nothing new he hasn't tried. I think we're in the clear from here on."

"Probably so," I agreed hopefully.

We should have known better. No coon ever runs out of things to try. Frosty hadn't, as we were soon to discover, for there *was* something new on the Kelly Ranch.

The week before, the lemon grove had been readied for the pickers. Roger and Hal had run a drive between every four rows of trees; the Sunkist Association had stacked boxes at the head of each row; just that morning the busload of Mexican-American pickers and their orange-colored ladders had arrived. Ever since breakfast we had heard the men singing and calling back and forth in Spanish. Who said there wasn't anything new on the ranch? There were, in fact, a number of things. Frosty found them all, one by one. Not fifteen minutes after the ladder incident, he came upon the green booth out at the far edge of the lemon grove.

What was this? He'd never seen it before, but no wonder. Being portable—and temporary—it hadn't been there since the last lemon picking, about three months earlier. But there it was now, door unhooked, ready for service—and a perfect booby trap. Scurrying among the startled workers, several of whom tossed their half-filled bags of lemons high in the air and bolted toward the road, Frosty all but collided with the green booth. And because the door responded so readily to his sensitive, safe-cracker touch, in he scooted.

Well, what do you know? The way these humans anticipate a coon's every want! Here in the lemon grove were the joys of the ranch house. Here was another Babbling Brook! With renewed zest for living the full life, he hurled himself at the familiar white oval and, in the doing, very nearly topped his performance on the high ladder. He did permanently cure himself of leaping before he looked.

Not accustomed to wild animals rushing around in their midst, lemon pickers were scattering everywhere, shouting *"Madre de Dios"* as they went, reverently pleading for their Maker to save them. But it was Frosty who needed saving, and it was David who did it. Before the coon succeeded in making a monumental outcast of himself, David grabbed him. Had Frosty tried this a month earlier, when he was smaller, he would have outlawed himself from the human world, and probably from the animal world as well.

As it was, we completed his utter humiliation for the day by scrubbing him outdoors, in an old-fashioned washtub, until we raised suds so high he couldn't see out. The strong soap stung his eyes and nose unmercifully, the disinfectant smell offended his dignity, and being dunked up and down like a pair of dirty socks shattered Frosty's estimate of his status in the family circle. It certainly gave him something to rise above, for he knew only too well that his halo had slipped.

Finally managing to free himself from our efforts to make him an acceptable member of society again, Frosty flopped out of the tub and onto the grass. In a cocoon of suds, he made for the orange grove, leaving a trail of mud in his wake. Under the long, friendly skirts of one of the trees he rolled himself dry, and nursed his hurt feelings, until once again everything in him cried out for love and attention. Then he came bounding across the irrigation furrows and rushed to us to be hugged and fussed over, just as if nothing unusual had ever happened. And when he did, the scamp, we scratched his ears and let him chew on our hands.

Afterwards, in the house, we laughed when he mussed our hair, and even when he squeaked the cupboard doors. In remembering the poor, trapped coon in town, we were grateful to the point of tears that his soft, little hands were whole, so that he could.

16

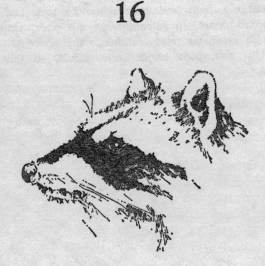

FROSTY'S BIG DAY came on a Saturday, about the middle of January, when he had a very special caller. One of his oldest and best friends came to see him. Big Basin ranger Bill Weatherbee and his wife Dee, on a vacation trip south, stopped at the ranch, and what an uproarious reunion we had!

In the first place it was all such a surprise. Since we were off the beaten path, we seldom had visitors from redwood country up north. As we opened the door and saw Bill and Dee standing there, our cries of welcome brought Frosty on the double from the den, where he had been pestering Blackie. When he saw Bill, he rushed him and nearly mowed him down. But you don't mow Bill down quite that easily: he's over six feet tall, and hefty too. His big, booming voice was a bell-ringer for Frosty; it brought back memories of happy times. Bill had hardly stepped into the front room before he and Frosty were at it on the floor— rolling and tumbling and growling at each other like two fierce things bent on each other's destruction.

Dee, Ethel, and I sat down to visit and watch the roughhouse that was to absorb Bill and Frosty for most of the evening. It was good to be together again. For Frosty it was Heaven. Tuffy, with his stubby legs and long body built close to the ground, was no match for the coon, who was now approaching twenty pounds; their wrestling was a lopsided affair. But this giant of a man was someone he could really try his full muscle power on, and that he did. He gave Bill everything he had.

"I can't believe this is the same little fellow we had at the park," Dee laughed, watching Bill roll over with Frosty chewing on his neck and growling. "He must be nearly grown."

"He is," Ethel assured her, moving a chair back to give the main event more room. "And he's a very big coon—probably because he's been spoiled rotten. I guess he's had about everything his heart has desired."

"Do you have a cage for him?" Dee asked.

"He's never had a cage," I answered, "and never will. He's been free to come and go on the ranch, in and out, just like the cat and dog."

"Not even a collar?" she queried further.

Ethel shook her head. "He does have a harness and

leash," she replied, "just in case we need it sometime for something special. But I doubt that we'll ever use it."

Almost out of breath, Bill sat up to rest briefly and to roll up his sleeves. "Wow!" he puffed, "I can remember when not so long ago this was real easy. But now this guy is wearing me out. He's quick, and is he strong! Whew! I'm about winded. I haven't had such a workout since the Battle of the Bulge."

All evening the battle went on. Gradually Bill, for all his youth and vigor, began to slow down. Quick to sense an advantage, Frosty kept moving in to attack until, at last, even he began to stagger. But give up? Never. It was Bill who finally leaned against the couch and called it quits. Once more Frosty leaped at him, but this time his leap fell short; he had run out of zip, and he landed not on Bill, but on the rug in front of him.

After a moment Bill reached over, gathered the coon into his arms, and laid him on the couch; gently he pushed him against the jacket he had tossed there as he came in. Exhausted, Frosty sat quietly, panting just a little. He put his head back, content to let the warm coziness of the down-filled lining billow up around him as he began to scratch his head and his chest in his usual fight to stay awake. His eyes closed; limply his head fell forward on his chest. Swathed in utter peace, he sank deep into coon dreamland. There he sat, and for nearly an hour he didn't even move.

"He's going to be all right," Bill said meaningfully. We were now approaching the middle of January, and Frosty would soon leave us to take up his own life. Ethel and I nodded sadly. We were aware that mating season was near.

To get our minds off the separation we must inevitably face, Bill suddenly remembered that he'd been saving a Big Basin coon story for us. Wherever Bill went, he always took with him something funny to relate. He gave this one to us just as it happened, acting it out, sound effects and all, for that was his way. Both Ethel and I almost forgot our heartache as he launched into a colorful account of an incident that had taken place in the park after we left.

During the winter, he said, this coon had become quite friendly with the Wagners—one of the ranger families who lived up in Flea Protrero. The Wagners, it seemed, had bought a television set. This raccoon, like so many of today's forest folk who want their wilderness and modern luxuries, too, had taken to sitting on the front porch railing in order to look in through the Wagners' big window and see what was going on. All evening, every evening, she'd perch there, fascinated. As long as the Wagners stayed up to watch programs, so would the coon. Right along with her human family, she enjoyed Bob Hope, Disney cartoons, and Marshal Dillon—even the commercials. But there was one show to which she was allergic: Lassie. Whenever the collie came barking into view, she would jump down and run for timber as if a pack of hounds were snapping the rings off her tail. All the residents of the meadow thought this so hilariously funny that at the moment of Lassie's appearance, they would run to their windows so they could see Sally—as they called her—make a dash to safety.

Then one night, after Sally had been a TV addict for months, she became confused or frightened or sick—or something, no one in the meadow could figure out just what. The same programs she had been accustomed to watching were on; yet, for some reason, Sally couldn't seem to stay on the porch rail to see them. She kept jumping down and wandering disconsolately around the house, crying. She came as close as a coon could to

wringing her hands and moaning. Telephones all over
the meadow buzzed as rangers and members of their
families called each other about Sally's strange performance. Everyone tried to find out what ailed her.
No one could come up with any solution.

One of the older boys offered her his chocolate cake,
but she would have none of it; two little girls tried
grapes, but that didn't work; several of the rangers
collected a whole string of bright, shiny keys, and hung
them on the rail for her to play with, but she didn't
want any keys. Night after night the meadow was upset
by Sally's distress. Still, there wasn't anyone who knew
what to do for her.

It was Mrs. Wagner who discovered the awful truth,
and put things to rights. She got Sally back on the
railing in time for Perry Mason.

Earlier that evening, as Mrs. Wagner washed dishes,
she tried to think back to the events of the day when
all this started. Could it be that *they* had done something to cause it— "Just what were we doing all day
Monday?" she asked her young son, who was drying
dishes.

"Paul and I went hiking to Berry Creek Falls," he
replied. "We were late getting back for dinner, remember?"

Mrs. Wagner nodded, and thinking aloud, went on:
"Sis and Daddy went to town for some supplies. Well,
then, none of you could have done anything to upset
Sally, for you weren't even here."

"What did you do all day?" Bob quizzed.

"Well, let me see. In the morning I baked those
apple pies for the potluck; then I went out for a visit;
then after lunch I cleaned the living and dining
rooms."

"And changed the furniture all around," Bob put in
helpfully.

"Yes, changed the furniture around. I was tired of it the other way. I moved the tea table over by the hall door, and the Bell chair, the step table, and the floor lamp over by the front window. That's all, I guess, before time to start dinner. Surely none of these things would have——"

Here Bill paused in his storytelling. He loved to create suspense.

"Go on, Bill," I urged. "What happened next?"

Laughing with pleasure over our obvious enjoyment of his story, Bill continued with his account.

With a sharp gasp, Mrs. Wagner stopped talking. Quickly dropping her dishcloth in the dishwater, she hurried through the house and out the front door. There she leaned against the railing, where Sally had always sat and peered in through their big picture window. Of course! Why hadn't someone thought of this before? "Don! Bob! Sister! Come out here quick!" she called. "I've discovered what's wrong with our coon." And she had.

By the time her family had joined her on the front porch, she was laughing so hard she couldn't speak. Instead, she pointed toward the window. Not one of them could see the television program just then going on. The floor lamp was directly in the way.

Rushing indoors, Mrs. Wagner moved the lamp out of sight—to the other side of the chair—so there was once again clear viewing from the porch railing.

That night, and from then on, the meadow folk could look over at the Wagner front porch and see Sally sitting contentedly on her usual perch, completely absorbed in some wild west show or a safari into darkest Africa. All was well in the meadow once more.

His story told, Bill leaned back in his chair and

grinned happily. "That's about all the scuttlebut of any consequence from Big Basin," he laughed. "Just thought you ought to know what's going on with the coons you left behind. What the crew is doing isn't half as newsy."

On January 17, a few days after Bill and Dee left, we received a telephone call from the library in Santa Paula. The children's librarian, preparing to conduct a story hour that afternoon, wanted to know if we would bring Frosty in. "We have this new raccoon book," she said. "I thought I'd read it to the youngsters, and if you could bring your coon in so they'd be able to see a real, live one——"

"I think Frosty would like that," I said, winking at him as he looked up from leafing through the telephone directory. And so we made a date for 3 P.M.

I went to the den, got the harness and leash, and after a struggle finally had it on him. "We're going to town, you and I," I said. "You have an appointment with some children at the library. You are going to be a Big Shot."

Strangely, I don't think he even heard the magic words. Even if he did, they didn't have the appeal for him that getting rid of that dastardly girdle had. He tried every trick he knew to free himself of that contraption that held him in such a vise-like grip, and wouldn't let him go.

You might know I'd give up and take it off. In pure relief, a big smile lightened his face as he tore for the back screen door, hurled himself against it, and burst into the big out-of-doors.

"Well," I said to Ethel as we tossed the hated harness into the waste basket, "there goes a blithe spirit. We're not going to make him wear that rig—even to meet a roomful of children. I can't imagine what kind of a riot we're going to have at the library this afternoon, but it ought to be a head-splitter."

We needn't have worried. Frosty never kept his appointment. He had another one that was much more important. Sometime before the Children's Hour he went to meet someone else. And he never came back. For him the time had come to go wild.

17

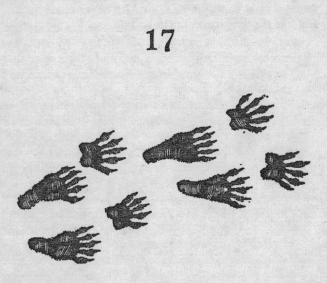

WE HAD EXPECTED something like this to happen, and we were sure it wouldn't be long until it did. All signs pointed that way—such as the opened and pilfered garbage cans of the neighbor ranchers; the half-eaten oranges, found farther and farther away from the house as the days passed; the hand and foot prints in the mud of the deep barranca that bordered the eastern edge of the Kelly acreage. Frosty had been staying out later and later at night, too, sometimes not asking to be let in until almost day break. Once, shortly before his date at the library, he didn't come for breakfast until the middle of the morning.

"We won't have Frosty much longer. Better get used

to the idea," I told Ethel, as we watched him curl up for a nap after his night out.

"Maybe he just wants to hibernate," she suggested. "After all, it is winter."

"And this is California," I reminded her. "Lowland coons in California have been known to sleep out a few dark rainy days, but that's all. He could have done that before now, but he never has. No, this sleepiness isn't that at all."

Frosty had always been free to go whenever he wished, and we were not holding him now. We knew that one day the call of the wild would command him to return to his own kind. We also knew that when it did, he would go, no matter how much he loved us. He wouldn't be able to help himself. People who raise a wild animal must face this sometime, or be guilty of imprisoning their pet—of denying him the freedom they prize so highly, and demand for themselves. Such a thing is unthinkable to those who claim to be decent and civilized and believe in the Golden Rule.

When Frosty didn't turn up in time to keep his library engagement that morning, I called the librarian and explained the situation. "You can tell the children," I said, "that our raccoon has probably gone to set up his own home."

Still, we weren't quite sure. Perhaps Frosty hadn't gone to seek a mate after all. Perhaps he had met with an accident or had gotten himself into some new dilemma and was waiting to be rescued. It would be just like him. We had to know, so we started out to see if we could find him.

Leaving the unsuspecting Tuffy gnawing on a bone in the front yard, Ethel and I walked through the walnut grove toward the barranca. We hunted around among the scattered brush there for some time before we found those baby-like hand and footprints we loved so much. "They're headed toward the river," I said, knowing that this would be true.

That's where they went, all right, although not directly. Just beyond the windbreak of tall eucalyptus trees that marked the lower end of the Kelly orange grove, there was a slight detour. It was caused by other coon footprints coming out of the adjoining ranch and down into the barranca. At that point, there appeared to have been considerable milling around, for the tracks circled each other several times before they continued downslope—together.

"Enter the heroine," Ethel said, noting that the other prints were smaller than Frosty's.

"Sure looks that way," I laughed. "Well, let's follow them."

We did. We followed those coon footprints down the barranca toward the bottom of the valley, to the damp sands of the riverbottom willow jungle. But there they mingled with the prints of all the other coons who lived along the stream, and were lost. No longer could we find any that we could identify as Frosty's. After seven months we had come to the end of the line.

Realizing now that we would probably not be seeing Frosty any more, neither Ethel nor I could talk. Instead, we poked around among the trees and bushes for over an hour. We tried every way we could to postpone hiking back to the ranch, for whenever we did start back it was going to mean returning to a home that would never again know Frosty's bubbling presence. As I dabbled in the water, ran my hands over the rough bark of the cottonwoods, and picked up pretty rocks here and there, I had to keep reminding myself that this was the moment we had been building for; that this was the event that Gary and I had talked about with such happy anticipation on the day he brought the orphaned Frosty to my cabin in Big Basin. This was Graduation Day.

For a long time Ethel and I sat among the riverside grasses and listened to the sounds of the woodland. The songs of many birds filled the air. But it was the soft gurgling of water, eddying around some rocks and lapping gently against the streambank, that held my attention. I couldn't help remembering those afternoons at Big Basin when Frosty and I explored Opal Creek together. All that we had heard then were the birds and the soft movement of water on its way to the sea—just as this was. But his soft hands had discovered much more, for they were his eyes, and they saw into a world I would never know. How busy they had been as they delved into quiet pools and frothing riffles, and brought out a multitude of little squirming things.

Leaning over a dark pond at my feet, I saw that this water, too, teemed with all the creatures so dear to every coon heart. And, as I looked around me, I saw no lack of hollow trees and thickets where two young coons could begin life together.

On both sides of the valley, the rolling hills, only recently soaked by generous rains, were slowly becoming as green and beautiful to roam upon as the emerald hills of Ireland. Even the afternoon breeze from the ocean was friendly in the playful way it tossed last autumn's cottonwood and sycamore leaves lightly among the new grasses. It just seemed to me that Nature couldn't have been more kindly than she was at that moment for this very special occasion.

Sitting there with a lump as big as a tennis ball sticking in my throat, I wondered if Frosty's mate would have to teach him how to kill. And I thought of all the things he could teach her, and of all the adventures he had had that he could share with the other coons who had never been around human people or inside their homes.

As he fingered the riffles yonder, for instance, he could describe his own private brook up there in the big house. He could explain how it worked and how he had been able to make it swirl and churn anytime he wished—for it knew no drought.

From Frosty, the poor underprivileged coons of the riverbottom would learn about fantastic, snorting monsters, such as tractors and trucks, and how one could go places in them without using legs. From him they would hear about blowtorches, bathtubs, and zippers; about jewelry boxes full of sparkling trinkets to hide and of all the wonderful places you could hide them.

Our coon would be sure to tell them about Scottie dogs you could easily outwit and about black cats who had a nasty way of hooking your sensitive nose with their sharp claws. And of course he would describe many other things of the ranch house, like the expensive French perfume he had filched and used much too profusely, the pianos he had played, the vacuum cleaners he had fought, and the huge four-poster bed he had slept in every night. And when he ran out of such odds and ends as these, he could entertain them with exciting accounts of those two stormy nights, high on the roof of the house, when he had splashed in the eave troughs that were running full. He'd have no trouble holding them spellbound with his stories of the enchanted world he had known. Now who could possibly doubt that Frosty was destined to become a social lion down there in the riverbottom woodland?

We never saw our coon again, although we knew he came back a time or two. Something prowling in the hired man's tenthouse one night—something that wasn't frightened one bit by a stick of wood thrown at him. That was Frosty, all right. A mere chunk of lemon wood crashing onto his head wouldn't have turned him from anything he had made up his mind to do.

We called our neighbors and asked them to please be patient about overturned garbage buckets until Frosty could completely sever his ties with humankind. I also called the dairy owner down near the river and prepared him for the fact that Frosty might be around some night. And I said I hoped they wouldn't be too irritated if a few quarts of milk wandered away—or if they found a coon milking one of their Holsteins. Frosty hadn't taken his bottle since he had grown up, but he still liked milk and wouldn't hesitate to get some any way he could. Well, perhaps he wouldn't bother the dairy. By then, he may have looked upon milk as kid stuff. I didn't know.

I did know that Frosty was missed. After he left, the house was unnaturally quiet. Everything stayed put. No longer were we catapulted from naps by pulled window shades that suddenly flew to the top and flippity-flapped round and round the roller. Most of the words in our typed letters were spelled correctly at last. We knew what to expect from one minute to the next—and it wasn't any fun.

For several weeks, Tuffy lay in the yard, rarely eating, longing for his pal, eternally watching for a bear sort of fellow to come bounding out of the orange grove. In that time he gradually lost all interest in life. Finally, when he sickened, his grief and lack of will to live were probably the real cause of his death.

Unless you are willing to suspend some things from the ceiling, nail others to the floor, and sit on the rest, you should never have a raccoon around. Adding a Frosty to the family circle requires the sharpest of wits—and these are never sharp enough, even so. You need iron endurance, a tolerance of clowning at all hours, and a devil-may-care attitude about order and time. But most of all, you have to have a love for him that's big enough to let him go.

Gary, our coon had the time of his life. And I kept my pledge to you and to myself. Frosty is now among his own kind—where he belongs.